William N. Copley

See

Yourself

as

Lovers

See

You

Dorothy Iannone

Die Ausstellung SEE YOURSELF AS LOVERS SEE YOU nimmt Aspekte der Freiheit, Selbstbestimmung und der Ekstase körperlicher Liebe in den Blick und führt zwei international renommierte Positionen zusammen: William N. Copley und Dorothy Iannone. Erstmals werden die Arbeiten des Künstlers und der Künstlerin, die 1993 unter dem Titel BERLINER AMERIKANER (gemeinsam mit dem Fluxus-Künstler Emmett Williams) im Haus am Lützowplatz, Berlin, ausstellten, in einer Gegenüberstellung gezeigt. Im Werk beider Künstler*innen lassen sich spielerische Formulierungen von Freiheitlichkeit und die Würdigung des Alltäglichen ebenso erkennen wie der humorvolle Umgang mit wiederkehrenden Bildelementen, Symboliken, Narrativen und Text. In ihrer unbeschwerten Auseinandersetzung mit Geschlechter- und Rollenklischees, gesellschaftlichen Normen und dem damit verbundenen Kampf gegen Zensur führen Iannone und Copley aus, was zu jener Zeit oft verdrängt wurde. Zu Lebzeiten hatten sie nur wenige Berührungspunkte. Unabhängig voneinander entwickelten beide eine extrem konsequente Bildsprache, die Parallelen wie auch deutliche Unterschiede erkennen lässt.

The SEE YOURSELF AS LOVERS SEE YOU exhibition focuses on aspects of liberty, self-determination and the ecstasy of physical love from the perspective of two internationally renowned artists, William N. Copley and Dorothy Iannone. First brought together (along with that of Fluxus artist Emmett Williams) in 1993, in an exhibition entitled BERLINER AMERIKANER at the Haus am Lützowplatz, Berlin, their work is now shown here for the first time in direct juxtaposition. Playful formulations of liberty and the celebration of the everyday

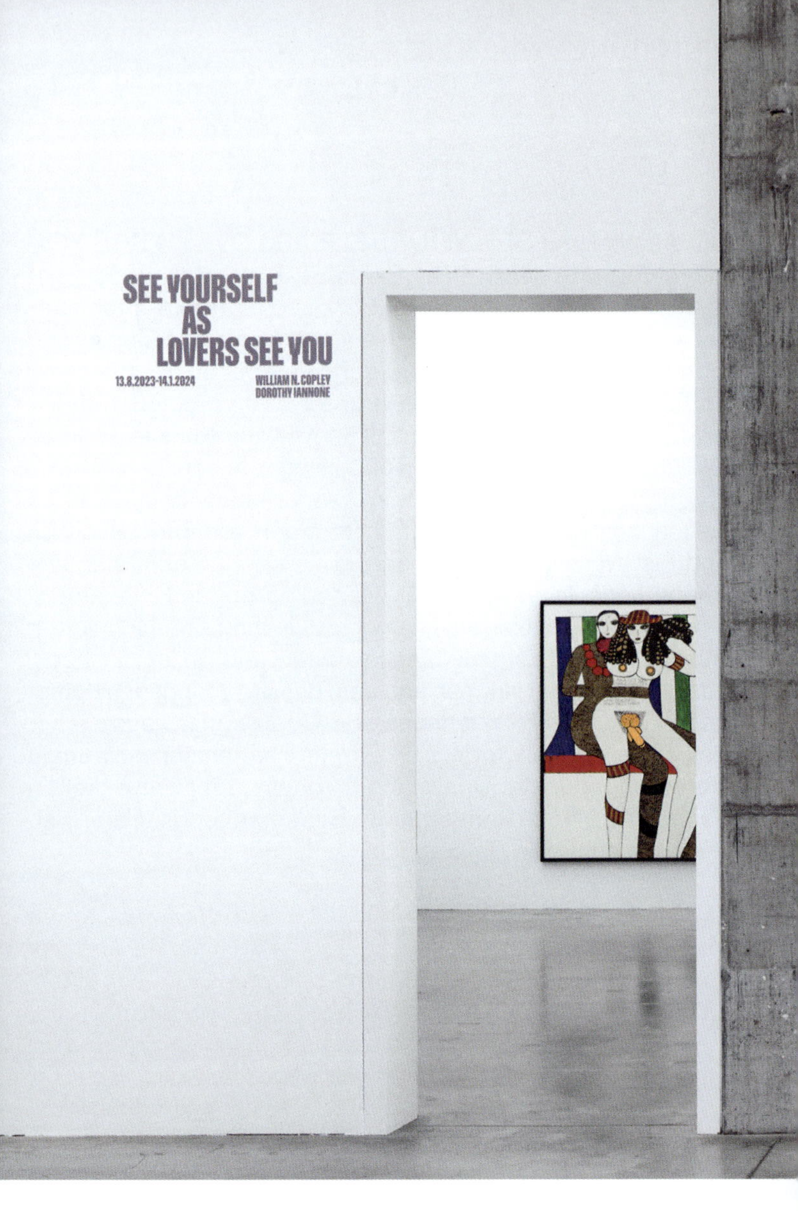

SEE YOURSELF
AS
LOVERS SEE YOU
13.8.2023–14.1.2024
WILLIAM N. COPLEY
DOROTHY IANNONE

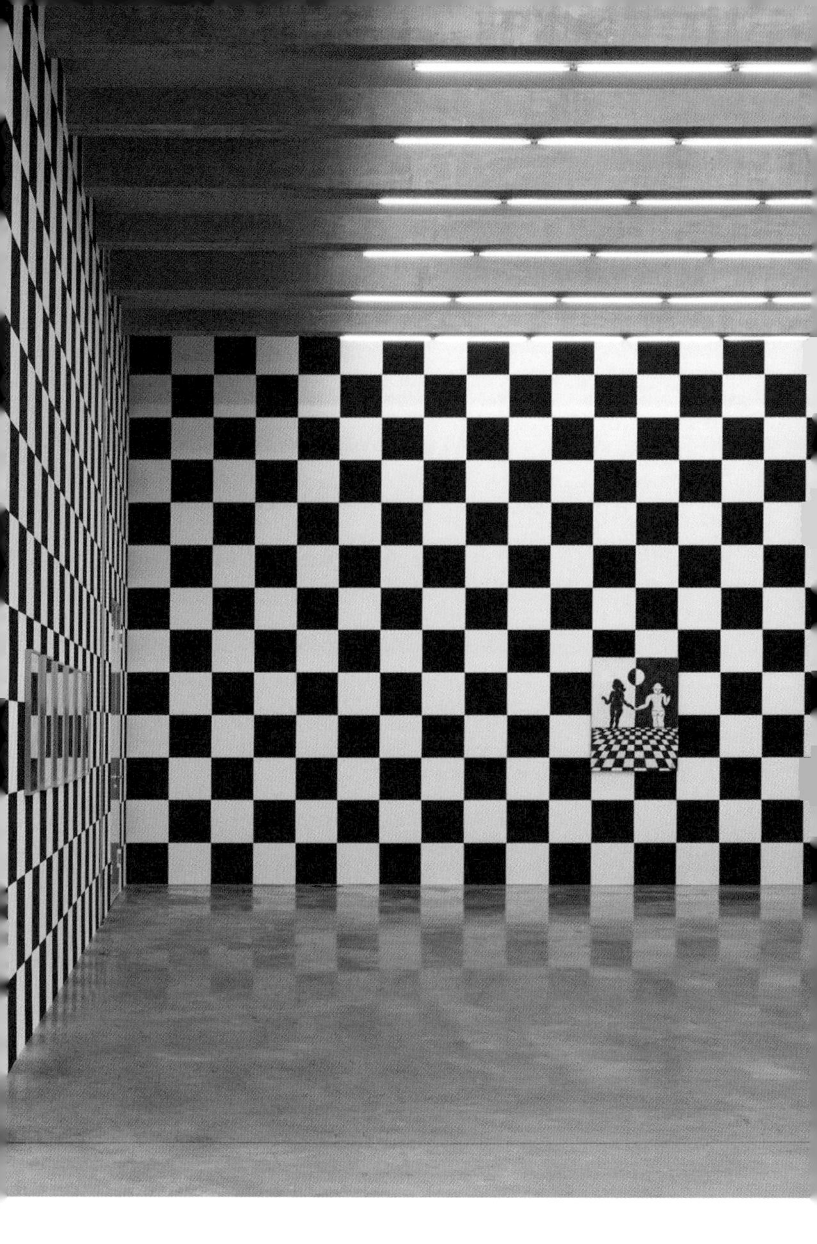

are coupled with humorous use of recurring pictorial elements, symbolism, narrative, and text. In their light-hearted interrogation of societal norms and gender and role stereotypes, and the resulting fight against censorship, they both gave expression to what had hitherto often been repressed. Copley and Iannone had only a few points of contact during their lives. Independently, they each developed their own extremely consistent visual languages, permitting recognition of both the parallels and the stark contrasts between their work.

In der Eingangshalle befindet sich die großformatige Wandmalerei *My Liberty (Red & Blue)* von Dorothy Iannone, gegenüber der zugehörige Text: „I Lift My Lamp Beside The Golden Door". Damit verweist sie auf die Freiheitsstatue und das ihr gewidmete Sonett *The New Colossus* (1883) von Emma Lazarus. Iannone zeigt das Wahrzeichen, auch „Lady Liberty" genannt, als kraftvolle, in schillernde Farben gehüllte überdimensionale Frauenfigur in mehreren Versionen, die Stärke ausstrahlt und gleichzeitig eine Träne vergießt. Gegenstück der Ikone ist *Lord Liberty*, ihr „Match" und ihre männliche Muse. Bewusst verknüpft Iannone in ihrem Werk das Thema der politischen Freiheit mit zutiefst persönlichen und autobiografischen romantischen Erzählungen.

In the entrance hall are works by Dorothy Iannone: two large-scale wall paintings, *My Liberty (Red & Blue)* and the text work *I Lift My Lamp Beside The Golden Door*, which reference the Statue of Liberty and a sonnet dedicated to her, *The New Colossus* (1883) by Emma Lazarus. Iannone depicts Liberty as a strong, larger than life-size, female figure in several iterations, all equally powerful and painted in vibrant colours, but shedding a single tear. Associated with her is *Lord Liberty*, both 'match' and muse for this iconic figure, and through whom Iannone links the theme of political liberty with the most profound personal and autobiographical romantic narratives.

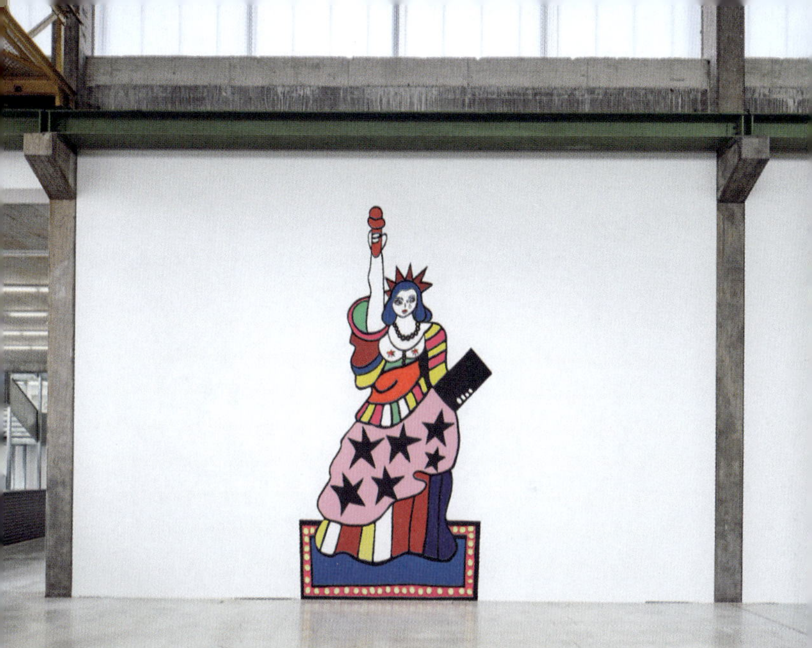

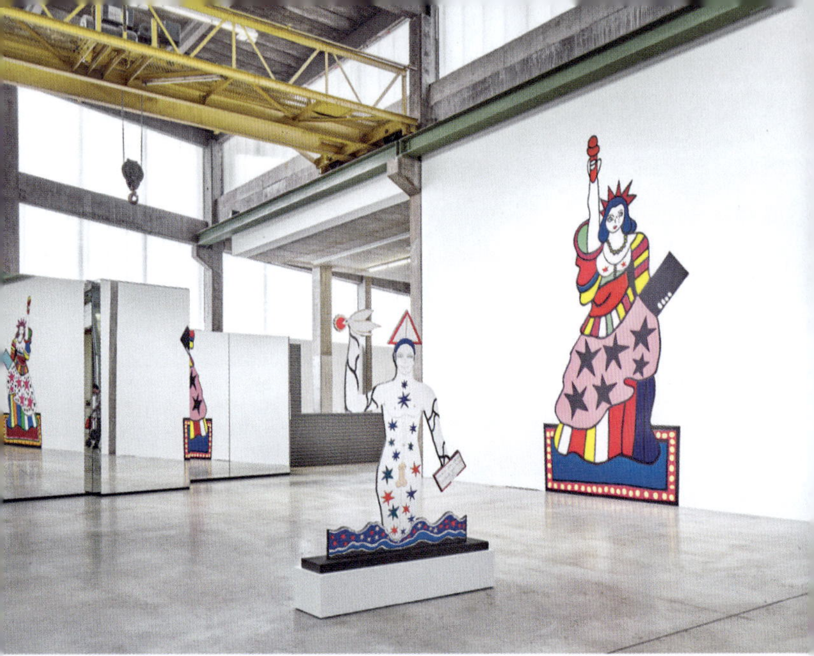

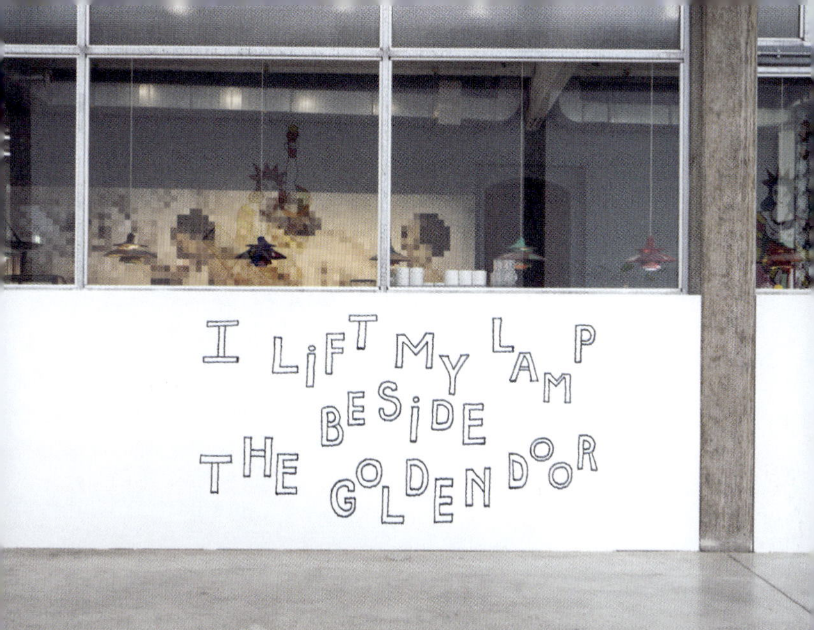

I LIFT MY LAMP
BESIDE
THE GOLDEN DOOR

Auch William N. Copley arbeitete sich kritisch an der amerikanischen Bildwelt ab, unter anderem an der Flagge der USA, die er wiederholt in Schwarzweiß ausführte und deren 50 Sterne, die für die 50 Bundesstaaten stehen, er durch das Wort „Think" ersetzte. Mit *Untitled (Lady's Lib)* aus einer Serie von übergroßen Briefmarkenzeichnungen verweist er auf die Frauenbewegung (Woman's Liberation Movement). In den Kohlezeichnungen dieser „Stamp Drawings" präsentiert er unter anderem die Namen von ikonischen Frauen wie Marilyn Monroe, Gertrude Stein oder Helen Keller neben holzschnittartig gezeichneten Männern.

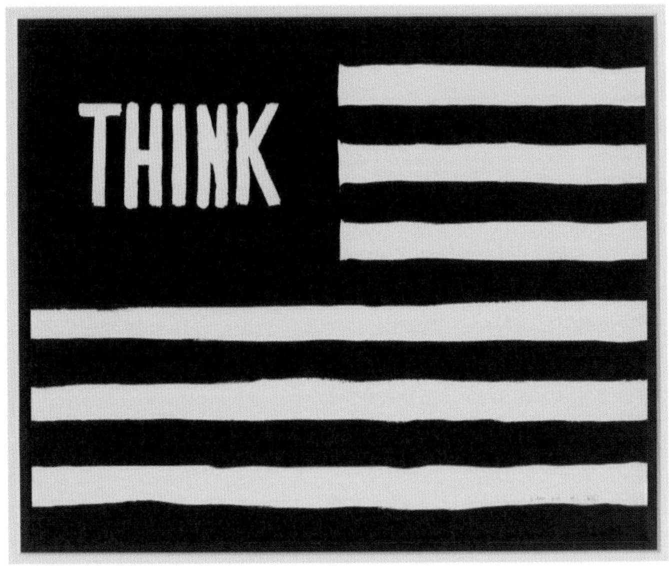

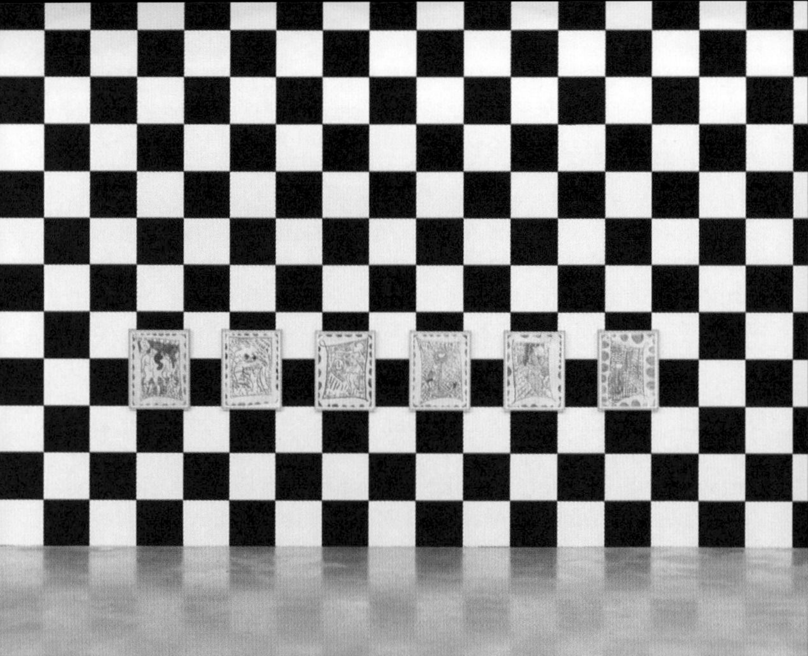

William N. Copley also engaged critically with American image-ry, including with the American flag, which he reproduced repeatedly in black and white, replacing its 50 stars, representing 50 states, with the word THINK. His *Untitled (Lady's Lib)*, one of a series of oversized postage-stamp drawings, references the women's liberation movement. In the charcoal drawings of the *Stamp Drawings* series, the names of iconic women, including Marilyn Monroe, Gertrude Stein and Helen Keller, are a thematic focus, as are men, drawn in the style of woodcuts.

Die Malerei *Outrageous Black and White* zeigt ein Paar, das unterschiedlicher nicht sein könnte und doch zusammenge-hört wie zwei Puzzleteile. Inspiriert ist es von Francis Picabias Werk *Die spanische Nacht* (1922), das Copley zeitweise besaß und dem er 1978 eine Serie von Malereien widme-te. Über Picabias Werk schrieb Copley: „Der Humor hier ist zart. Den Liebenden ist es egal, wie lächerlich sie aussehen. Könnte man diesen Bildern nicht einen anderen Namen geben als ‚Monster'?"[1] Copley verehrte den Exzentriker Picabia für sein freies Denken und das Ausbrechen aus kunsthis-torischen Schablonen. *Outrageous Black and White* steht exemplarisch für Copleys eigene Bildwelt, in der es feste Rol-len, Abläufe und viele schablonenhafte Figuren, sogenannte „stock characters", gibt. Angetrieben von dem Wunsch, sich als Maler wie ein Dichter mit Vokabeln in visuellen Bildern auszudrücken, schuf er Werke mit starker Symbolwirkung. Anders als Iannone überführt er erotische Chemie oftmals in Absurditäten. Die von Philara gewählte Szenografie des Schachbrettmusters ist wiederkehrendes Motiv bei Copley (z. B. in *Imaginary Game*) und verweist auf seine spielerisch überspitzten stereotypischen Geschlechterrollen, die sich auf die strategische Ebene eines Schachspiels übertragen lassen – ein interessanter Aspekt, wenn man bedenkt, dass die Dame im Schach die stärkste Figur ist.

The painting *Outrageous Black and White* depicts a couple who could not be more unlike, yet fit together like pieces in a jigsaw puzzle. The work is inspired by Francis Picabia's *The Spanish Night* (1922), which Copley previously owned and had explored in a 1978 series of paintings. On Picabia, Copley wrote, 'The humor here is tender. Lovers do not care how ridiculous they look. Might we not call these something else than "monster" paintings?'[2] Copley admired the eccentric Picabia's free-thinking attitude and his break with conventional art-historical templates. The painting *Outrageous Black and White* exemplifies Copley's own visual world, which encompasses set roles and sequences of events and is populated with template-like stock characters. Unlike Iannone, he often transforms erotic chemistry into absurdity. Driven by the desire to express himself as a painter in visual images, in the way a poet uses vocabulary, he created paintings with a strong symbolic effect. The chessboard pattern chosen by Philara for the exhibition scenography is a recurrent motif in Copley's work (in *Imaginary Game*, for example) and alludes to his playfully exaggerated gender stereotypes, which, if transposed to the strategic level of a chess game, become particularly interesting when one considers that the queen is the strongest piece in chess.

1 Estate of William N. Copley.
2 Estate of William N. Copley.

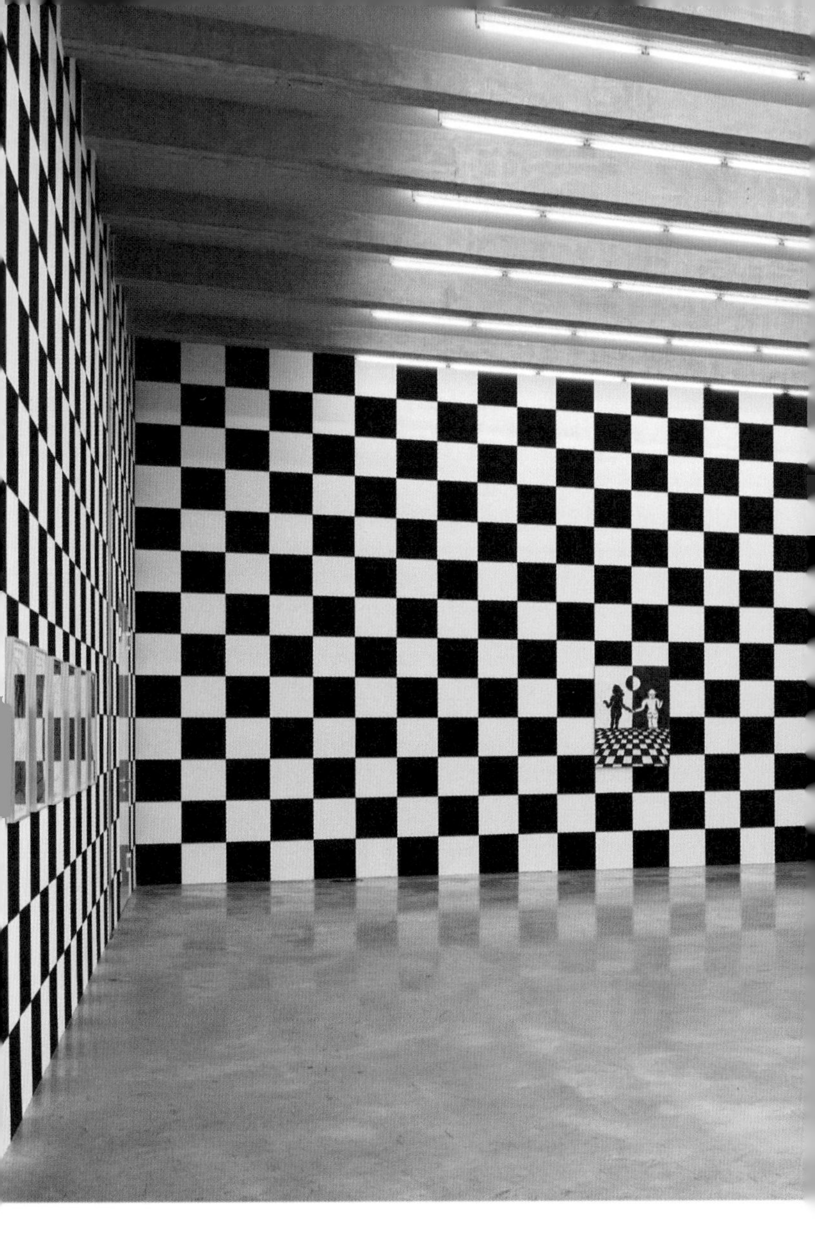

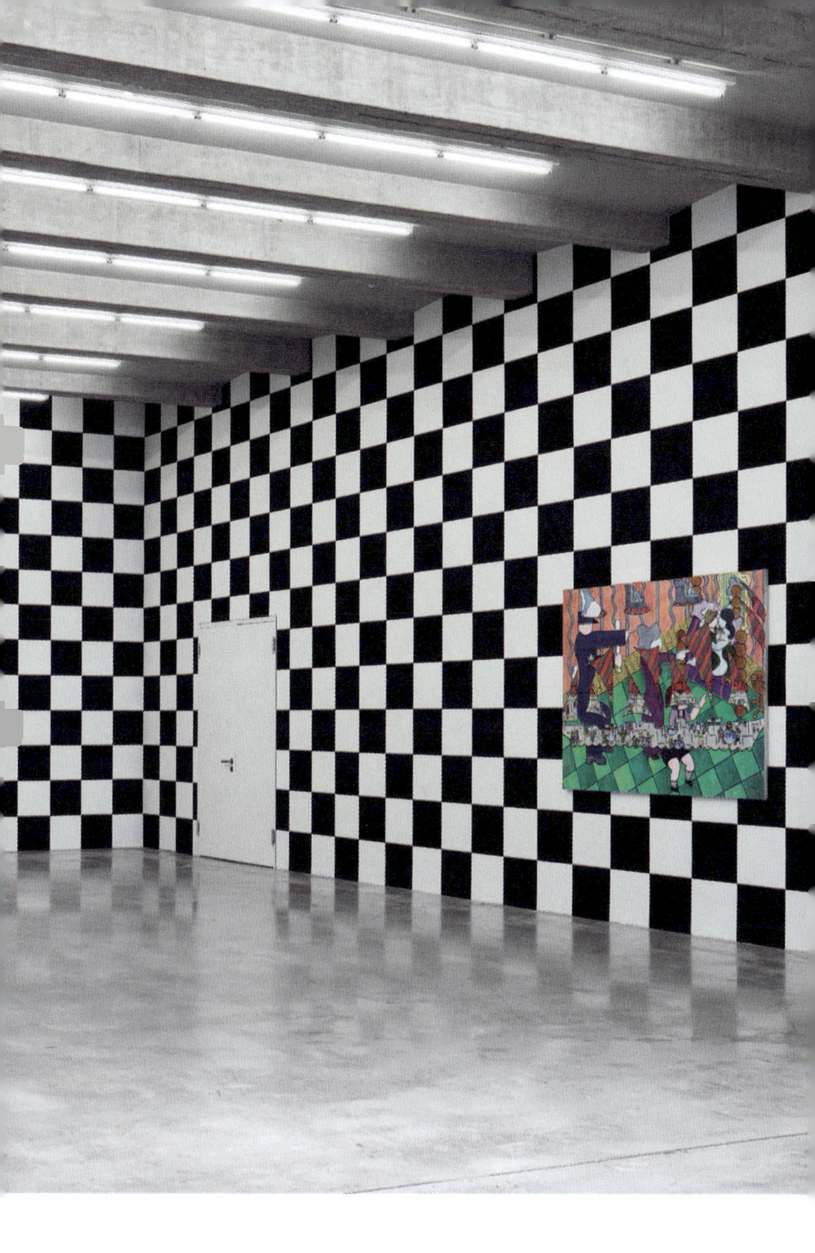

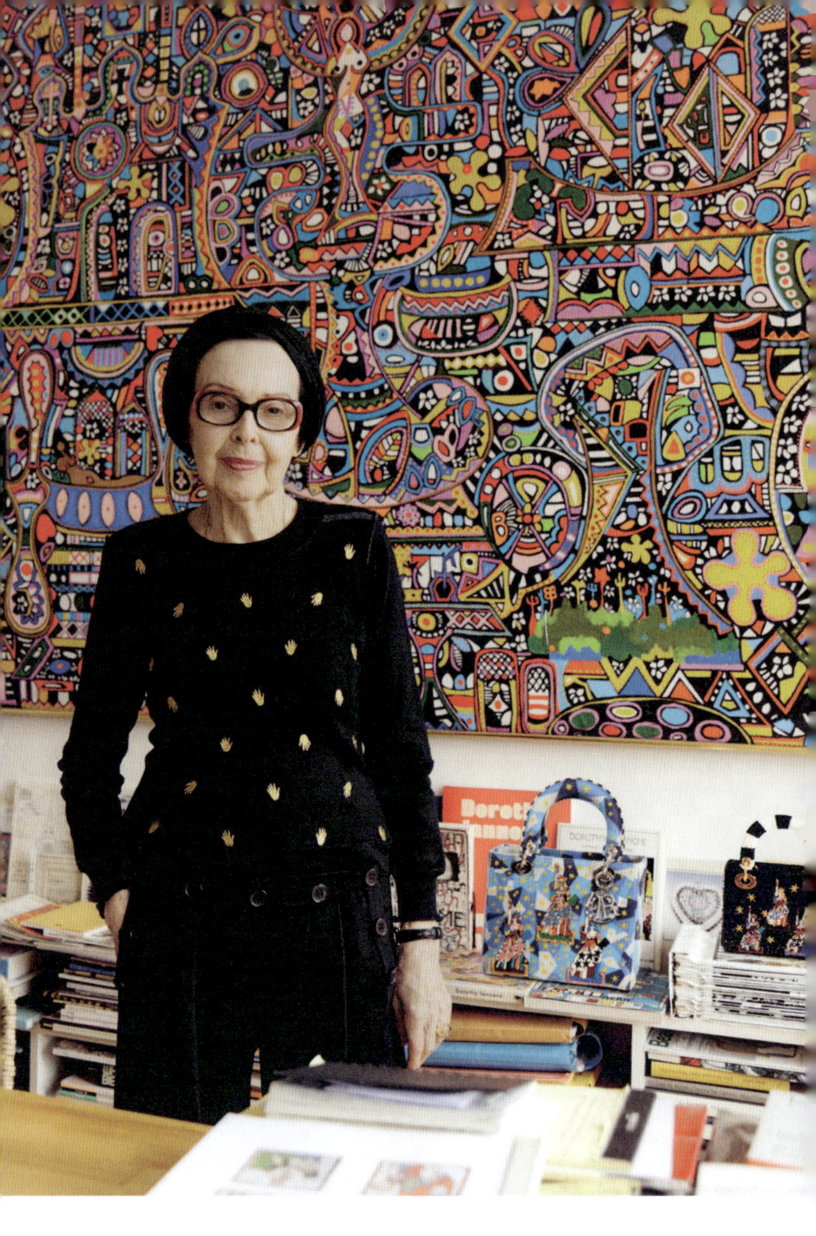

DOROTHY IANNONE

Während Copley vom Dadaismus, Surrealismus und der Pop Art beeinflusst war, kam Dorothy Iannone über den amerikanischen Expressionismus, der in den 50er Jahren vorwiegend männlich geprägt war, zu ihrer eigenen Bildsprache. *Let Me Have Men About Me That Are Fat* (1966) ist eine frühe Arbeit von Iannone, die zwar noch den Hang zum abstrakten Expressionismus erkennen lässt, aber bereits einige der Figuren zeigt, die sich mit der Zeit in ihrem Werk herausbildeten und ihren persönlichen Stil ausmachen. Kennzeichnendes Merkmal ihrer Charaktere waren von Beginn an deren deutlich erkennbare Genitalien. Gelegentlich erscheinen in ihrem frühen Werk bereits Textanteile: Der Titel des Bildes etwa ist ein Zitat aus Shakespeares *Julius Caesar*. In Iannones Œuvre wird das starke Freiheitsbestreben der Künstlerin offenkundig, das sie auch in Bezug auf Literatur zeigte: 1961 verklagte sie erfolgreich die US-Regierung im Namen Henry Millers und erwirkte damit die Erlaubnis zur Einfuhr seiner Bücher. Diese Offenheit hinsichtlich erotischen, bei Iannone insbesondere weiblichen Begehrens setzt sich in ihrer Kunst fort. Ein Ausbrechen aus Gender- und Rollenklischees, gemessen an der Zeit ihrer Entstehung, ist kennzeichnend für ihre Bilder.

Um 1966 fertigte Iannone einige hundert Holzfiguren (*People*) von realen, historischen, mythologischen und fiktiven Personen an, stets mit den charakteristischen explizit ausgearbeiteten Geschlechtsorganen, selbst wenn die Dargestellten vollständig bekleidet sind. Zu den Motiven zählen etwa die biblische Figur des *David* und eine Frau (*Woman*), unter deren Armen männliche Geschlechtsteile hervortreten.

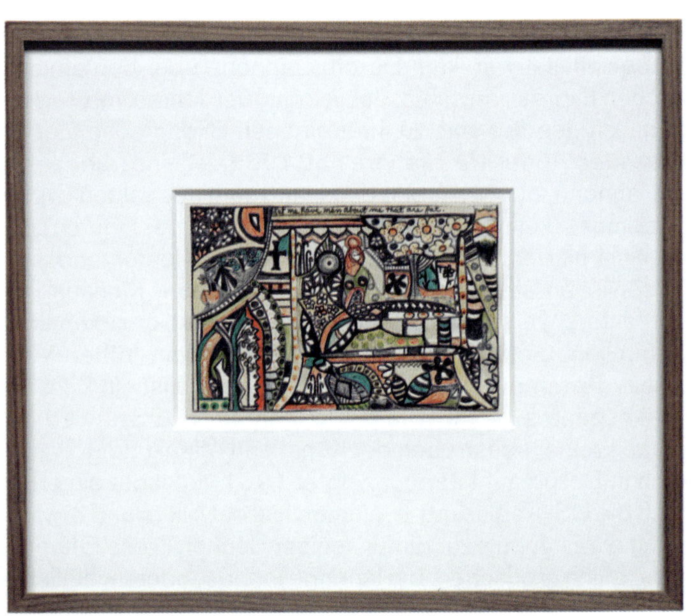
Let me have men about me that are fat.

While Copley was influenced by Dada, Surrealism and Pop Art, Dorothy Iannone arrived at her own visual language by way of American Expressionism, in the 1950s a predominantly male movement. While *Let Me Have Men About Me That Are Fat* (1966) (a quotation from Shakespeare's *Julius Caesar*), one of Iannone's early works, still leans towards Abstract Expressionism, one can nevertheless discern the individual figures that gained increasing importance in her work and the development of her own personal style. Even in her early figures, the genitalia are clearly recognisable, while fragments of text already occasionally appear. A powerful desire for freedom can be seen in Iannone's work, a characteristic which she had previously demonstrated in relation to literature. In 1961 she successfully took the US government to court on behalf of Henry Miller and gained the right to import his books. This openness to erotic desire and for Iannone, particularly female desire, carries through into her art. Viewed in the context of the time they were created, her pictures clearly show her breaking free from gender and role stereotypes.

Around 1966, Iannone made a few hundred wooden figures, entitled *People*, which represent real, historical, mythological, and fictional people, to all of whom she added characteristically explicit, visible genitalia, even when they were depicted fully clothed. Here, for example, are the biblical figure of *David* and an anonymous female figure (*Woman*), with male sex organs beneath her arms.

Bei uns (1969) ist ein Bild voller versteckter Objekte und persönlicher wie sexueller Anspielungen. Etwa ein Jahrzehnt lebte Iannone mit ihrem damaligen Partner Dieter Roth, der an der Kunstakademie lehrte, in Basel, Reykjavik und Düsseldorf. Dort schuf Iannone dieses Werk, das die private Wohnung, Sexualität und Liebe des Paars ins Öffentliche trägt. Ebenfalls hier entstand *Danger In Düsseldorf (Or) I Am Not What I Seem* (1973), eine Liebeserzählung über die fiktiven Figuren Otto und Anna Hase, die für Iannone und Roth stehen. In einer

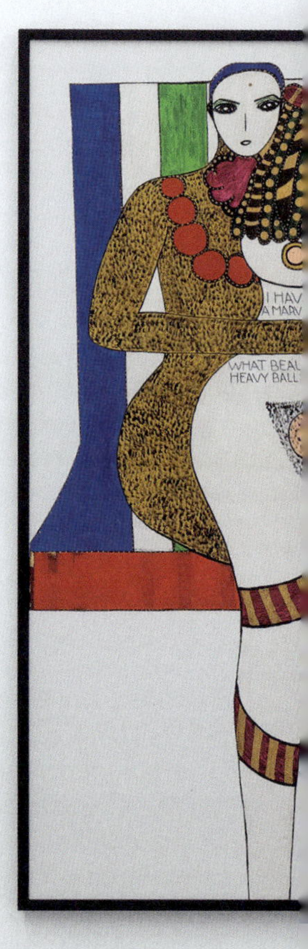
I HAV
A MARV
WHAT BEA
HEAVY BALL

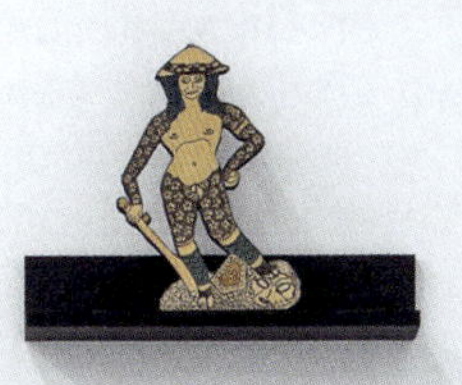

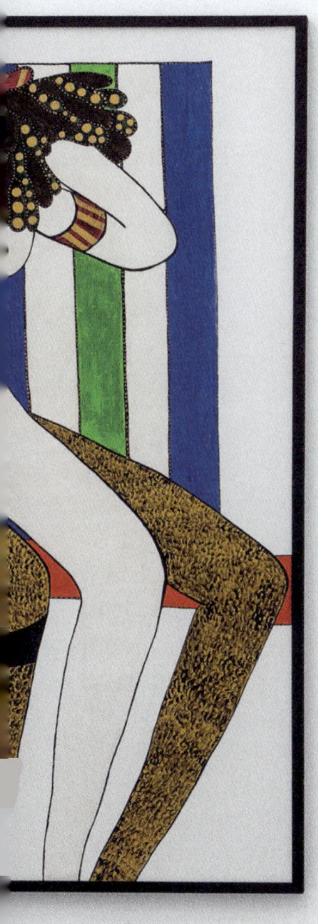

komplexen Bildaufteilung erzählt *Lions For Dieter Rot The Present Lion Master* (1971) die erotische Liebesgeschichte eines Paars in der Wildnis, das Löwen durch Musik zähmt. Die tiefe Verschränkung von Text und Bild im Werk von Iannone ist hier unverkennbar. *Miss My Muse* (2000) hingegen blickt zurück auf ihre Beziehung zu Roth (1930–1998) lange nach der Trennung der beiden.

Bei uns (1969) is a work that depicts hidden objects replete with personal and sexual allusions. For some ten years Iannone lived with her partner at the time, Dieter Roth, in Reykjavik and Basel, and in Düsseldorf, where Roth taught at the Kunstakademie. This work, which brought their private living space, sexuality and love into the public sphere, was made in Düsseldorf. It was here too that she created *Danger In Düsseldorf (Or) I Am Not What I Seem* (1973), a love story about Anna and Otto Hase, pseudonyms invented for Iannone and Roth. *Lions For Dieter Rot The Present Lion Master* (1971) narrates the erotic love story of a couple in the wilderness, along with wild lions that have been tamed by music. Its complex divisions make clear the close integration of text and image in Iannone's work. In contrast, *Miss My Muse* (2000) looks back on their relationship long after it had ended and after the death of Roth (1930–1998).

Neben männlichen Künstlern wie Roth, Joseph Beuys und Jean Tinguely war Iannones Werk in Düsseldorf zu dieser Zeit weit weniger präsent. Dennoch fand sie gerade dort zu ihrem eigenen Stil, nachdem sie sich in den USA das Malen beigebracht hatte. Sie bezeichnete Roth wiederholt als ihre persönliche „Muse" – ein Ausdruck, der sonst hauptsächlich von männlichen Künstlern in Bezug auf Frauen verwendet wurde. Auch nach der Trennung bleiben Liebe und sexuelles Begehren Mittelpunkt ihrer Arbeit. Impuls ihres Schaffens ist die Sehnsucht nach absoluter Liebe, die sie später in sich selbst suchte.[1] Auch zur Stadt Berlin, wo die Künstlerin ab

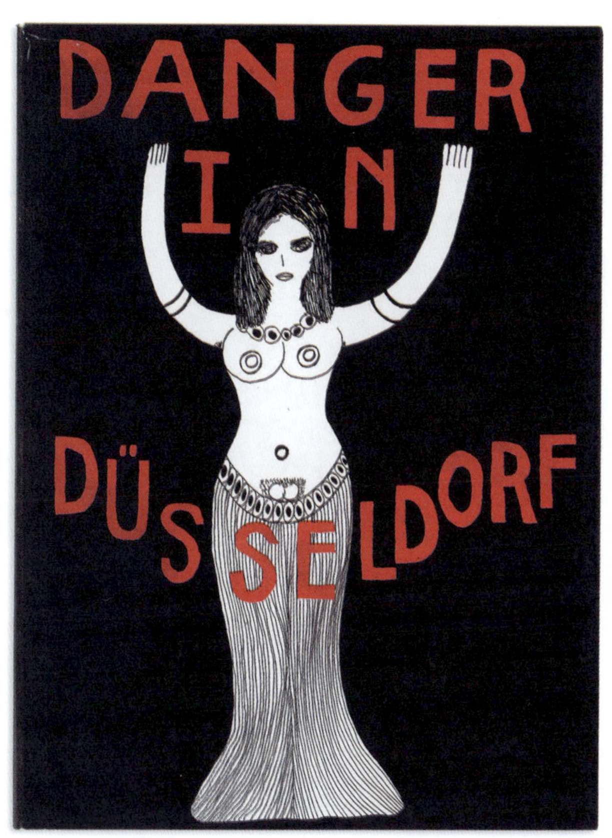

DANGER
IN
DÜSSELDORF

1976 lebte, entwickelte Iannone eine tiefe Verbundenheit. Bis zu ihrem Tod im Jahr 2022 blieb die Stadt ihre Wahlheimat. Anders als bei Copley steht in Iannones Arbeit die Liebe als Inspiration, als kosmologische, spirituelle oder empathische Weltumarmung im Fokus, ganz im Sinne von *Love Is Forever Isn't It.*

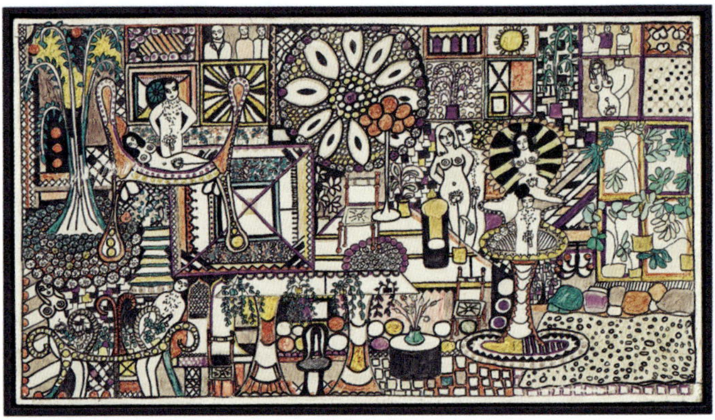

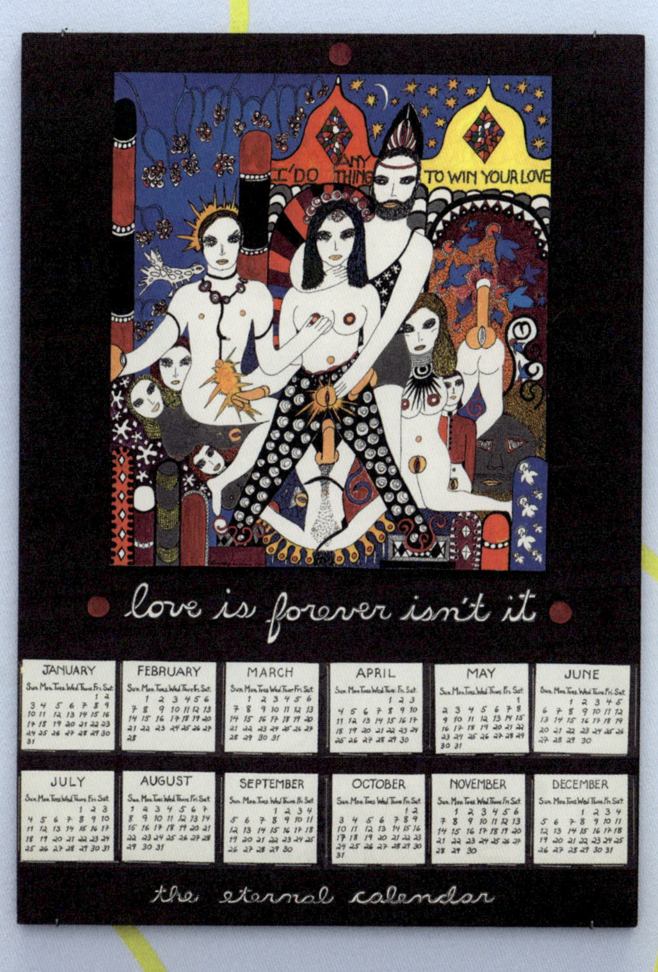

I'DO
ANY THING
TO WIN YOUR LOVE
love is forever isn't it
JANUARY
FEBRUARY
MARCH
APRIL
MAY
JUNE
JULY
AUGUST
SEPTEMBER
OCTOBER
NOVEMBER
DECEMBER
the eternal calendar

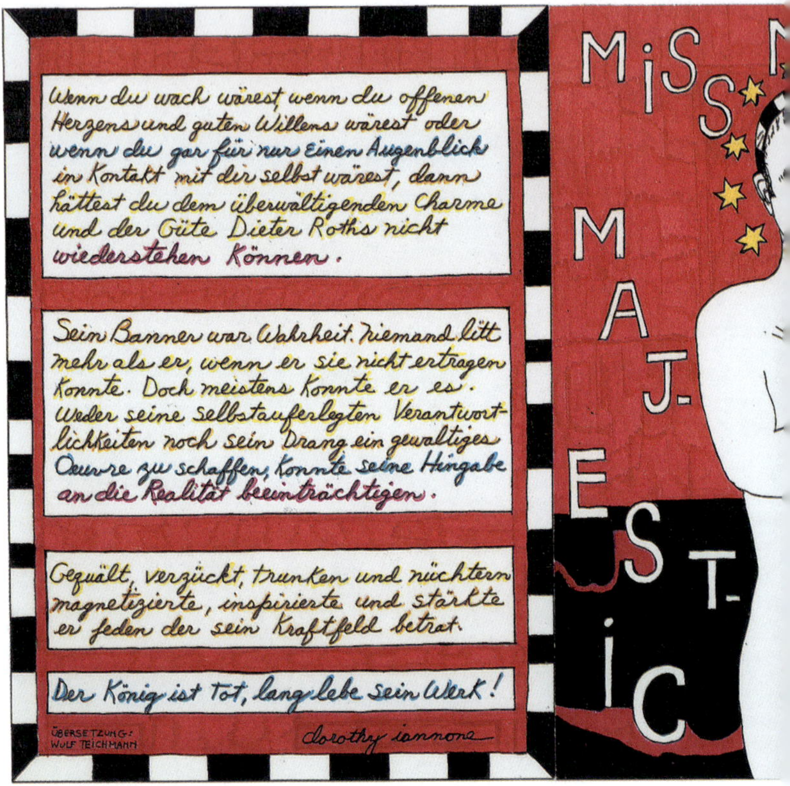

Wenn du wach wärest, wenn du offenen
Herzens und guten Willens wärest oder
wenn du gar für nur einen Augenblick
in Kontakt mit dir selbst wärest, dann
hättest du dem überwältigenden Charme
und der Güte Dieter Roths nicht
wiederstehen können.

Sein Banner war Wahrheit. Niemand litt
mehr als er, wenn er sie nicht ertragen
konnte. Doch meistens konnte er es.
Weder seine selbstauferlegten Verantwort-
lichkeiten noch sein Drang ein gewaltiges
Oeuvre zu schaffen, konnte seine Hingabe
an die Realität beeinträchtigen.

Gequält, verzückt, trunken und nüchtern
magnetisierte, inspirierte und stärkte
er jeden der sein Kraftfeld betrat.

Der König ist tot, lang lebe sein Werk!

ÜBERSETZUNG:
WULF TEICHMANN

dorothy iannone

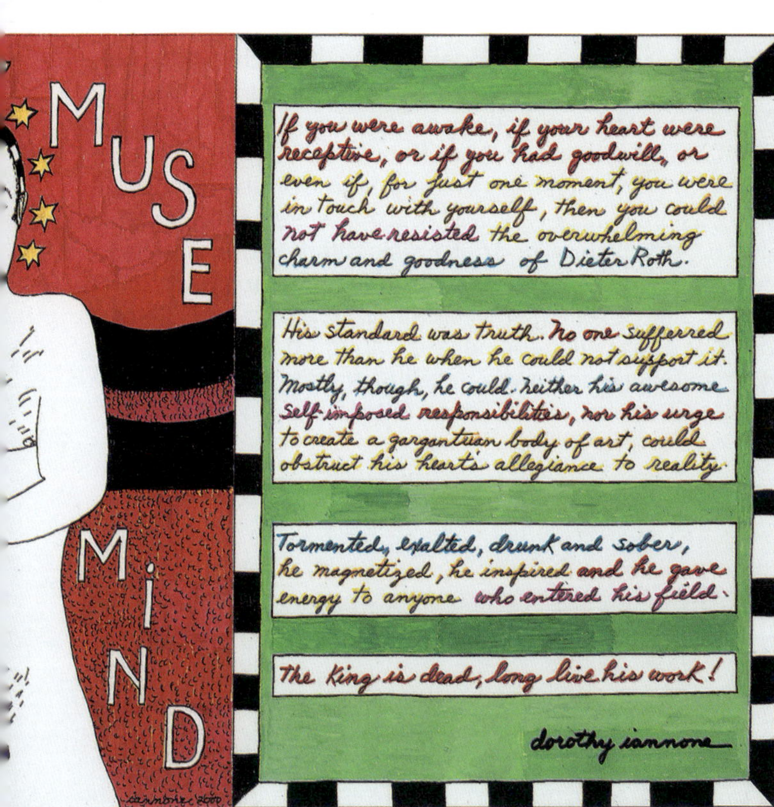

MUSE
MIND

If you were awake, if your heart were receptive, or if you had goodwill, or even if, for just one moment, you were in touch with yourself, then you could not have resisted the overwhelming charm and goodness of Dieter Roth.

His standard was truth. No one sufferred more than he when he could not support it. Mostly, though, he could. neither his awesome self-imposed responsibilities, nor his urge to create a gargantuan body of art, could obstruct his heart's allegiance to reality.

Tormented, exalted, drunk and sober, he magnetized, he inspired and he gave energy to anyone who entered his field.

The King is dead, long live his work!

dorothy iannone

1968 wurde Dieter Roth eingeladen, an der sechsten Ausgabe der von Copley herausgegebenen Publikationsreihe *Shit Must Stop*, kurz *S.M.S.*, teilzunehmen. Er trug eine Arbeit bei, die aus vier Karten bestand, die einer Schokolade beigelegt werden sollten. Im Anschluss lud Copley auch Dorothy Iannone ein, eine Editionsausgabe für *S.M.S.* zu realisieren. Hierfür entwarf sie *LBJ*, eine Darstellung des Präsidenten Lyndon B. Johnson, dessen Geschlecht provokativ aus seinem Anzug ragt. Leider wurde *S.M.S.* vor Erscheinen der Edition von Iannone noch im selben Jahr wieder eingestellt. Eine Postkarte von Dieter Roth an Copley zeugt von der Bitte um Rücksendung des originalen Designs an ihre Düsseldorfer Adresse, die vermutlich kurz darauf erfolgte.

In 1968 Dieter Roth was invited to contribute to the sixth issue of *S.M.S.*, short for *Shit Must Stop*, a series of portfolios published by Copley. He produced an edition of cards intended to accompany a chocolate bar. Copley subsequently also invited Iannone to contribute to an issue of *S.M.S.*, for which she created *LBJ*. This edition shows US President Lyndon B. Johnson with his sex provocatively depicted outside his suit. A note from the final issue of *S.M.S.* bears witness to the discontinuation of the *S.M.S.* series before Iannone's issue was to be published; a postcard from Roth to Copley asks for the return of her original design to her Düsseldorf address, which presumably happened shortly after.

1   „If the ideal lover will not appear, then I propose to become that person myself." Dorothy Iannone in: Dieter ROTH & Dorothy IANNONE, 2005, S. 159.
2   'If the ideal lover will not appear, then I propose to become that person myself.' Dorothy Iannone in: *Dieter ROTH & Dorothy IANNONE*, 2005, p. 159.

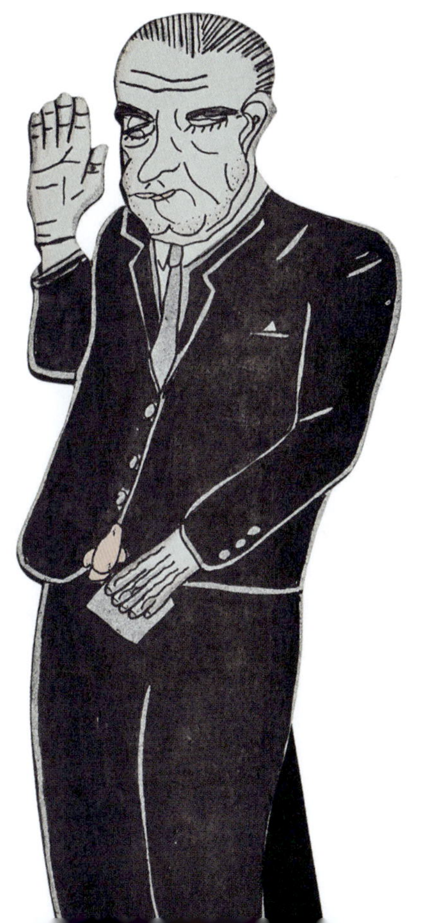

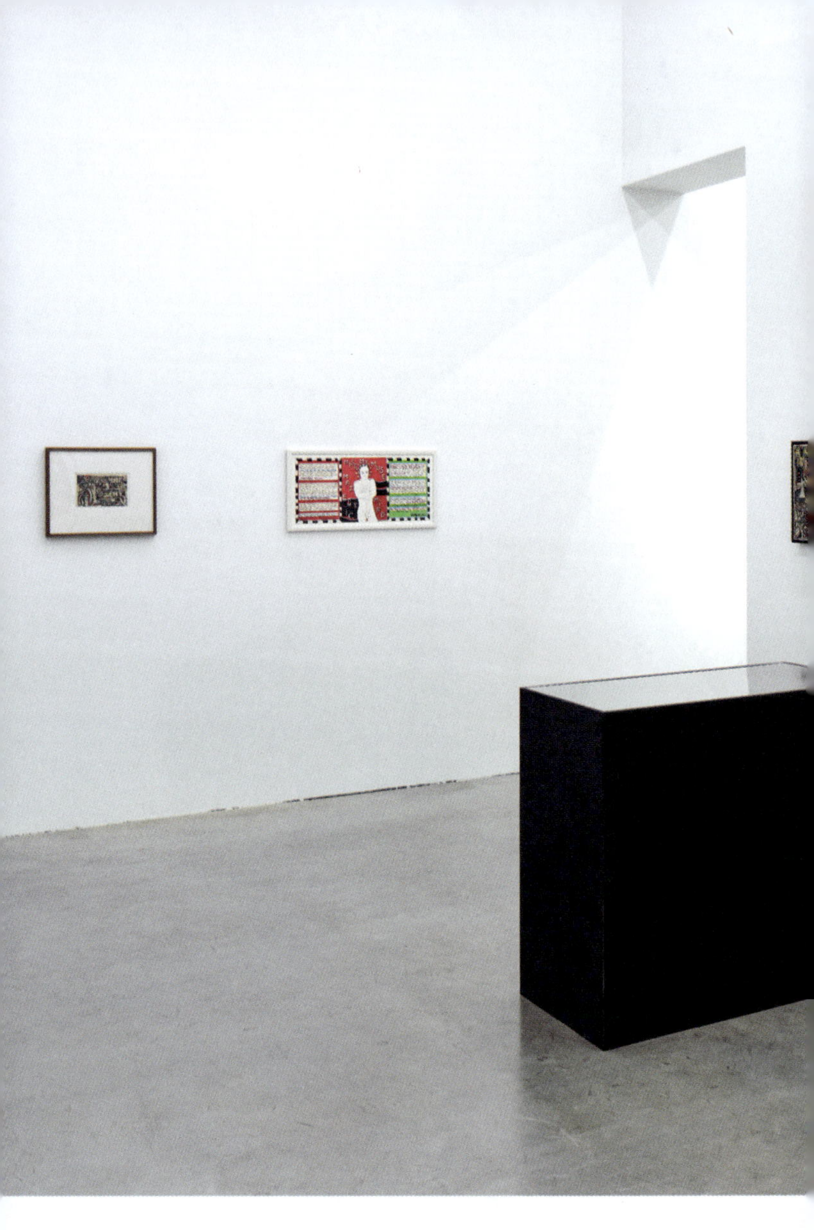

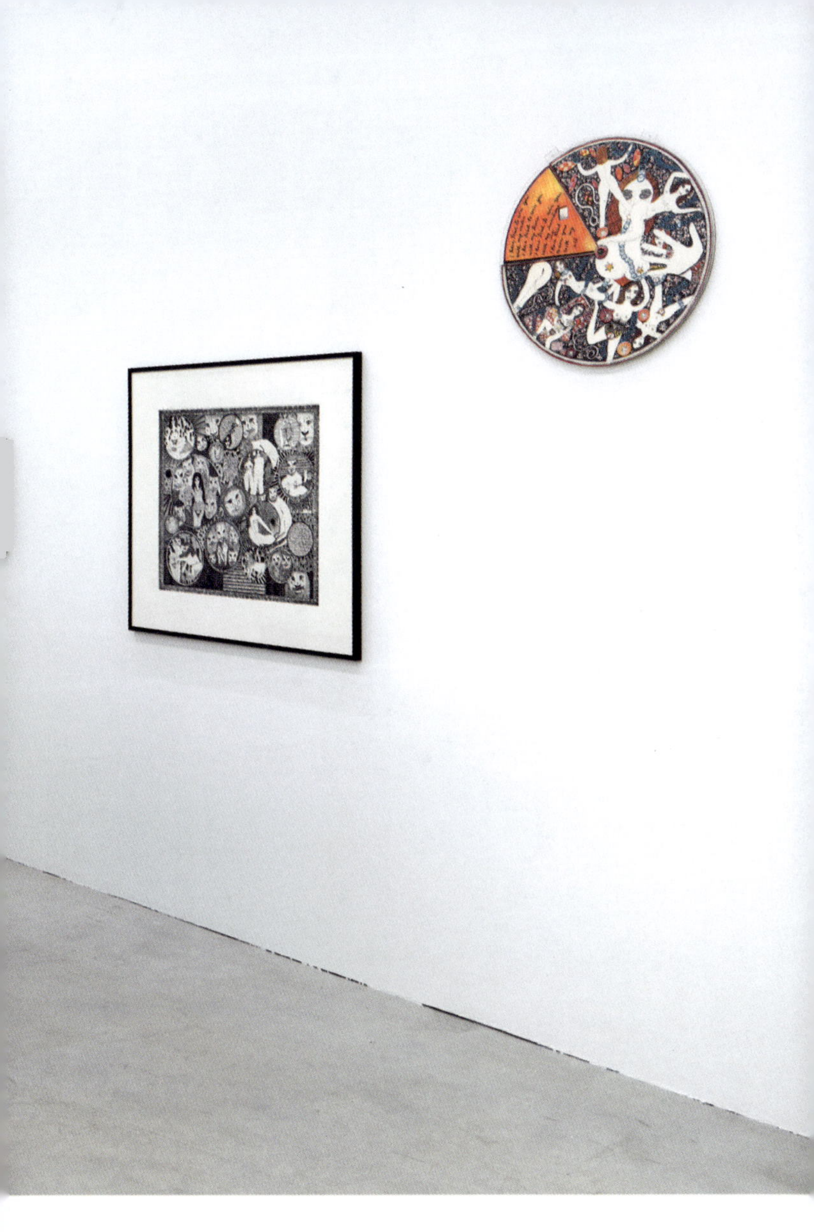

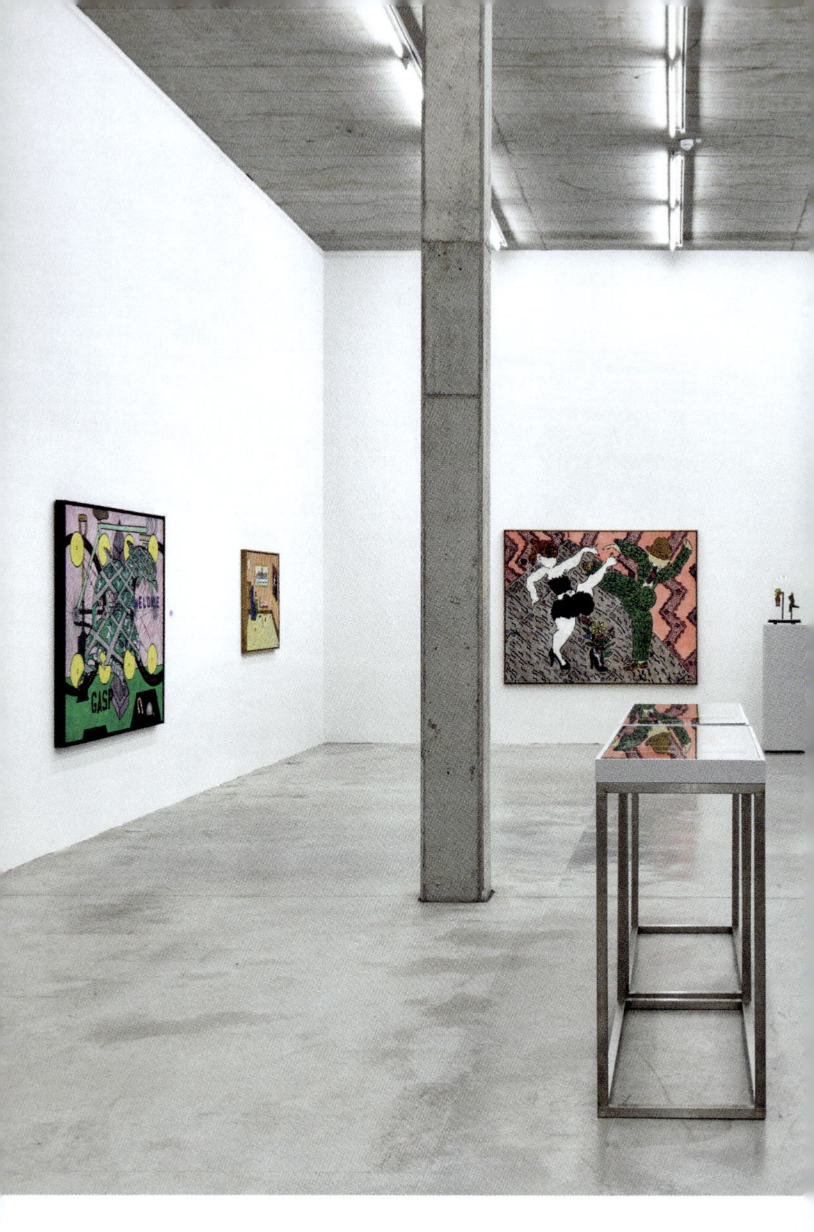

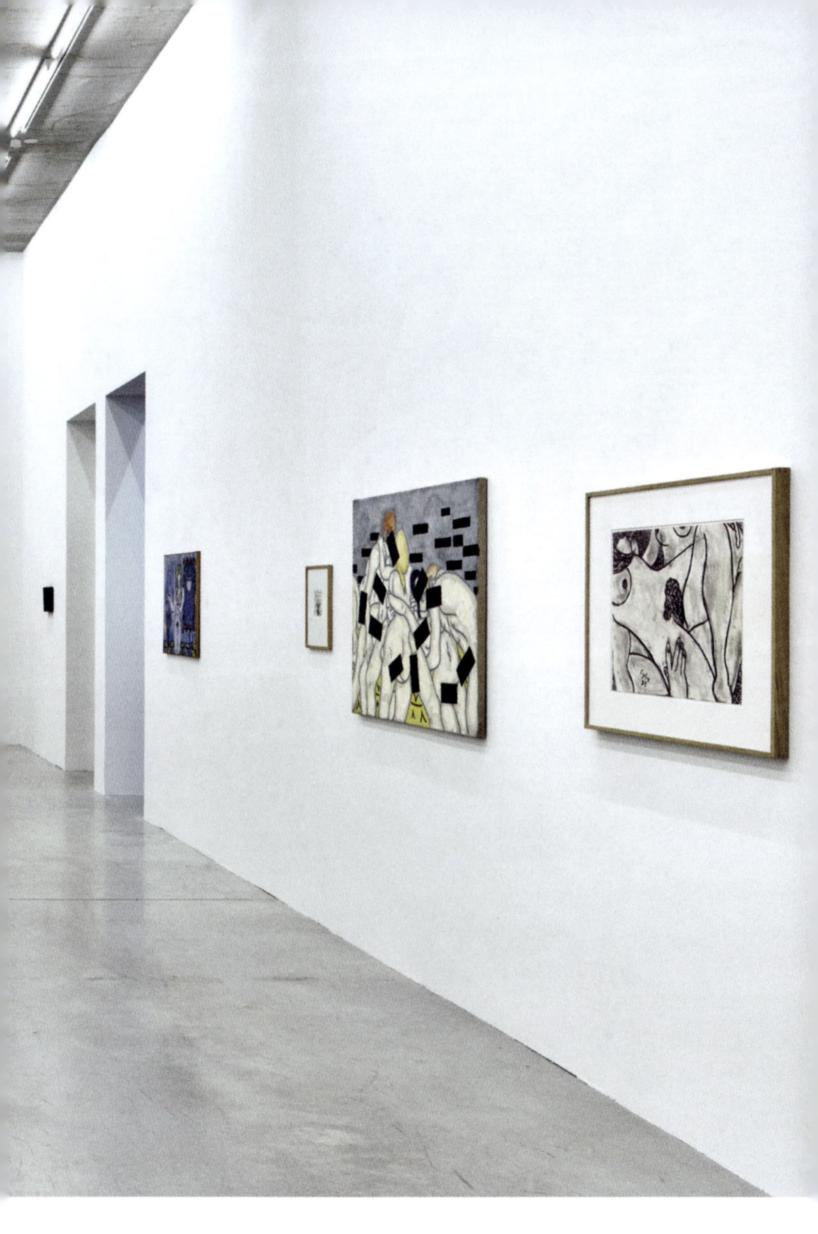

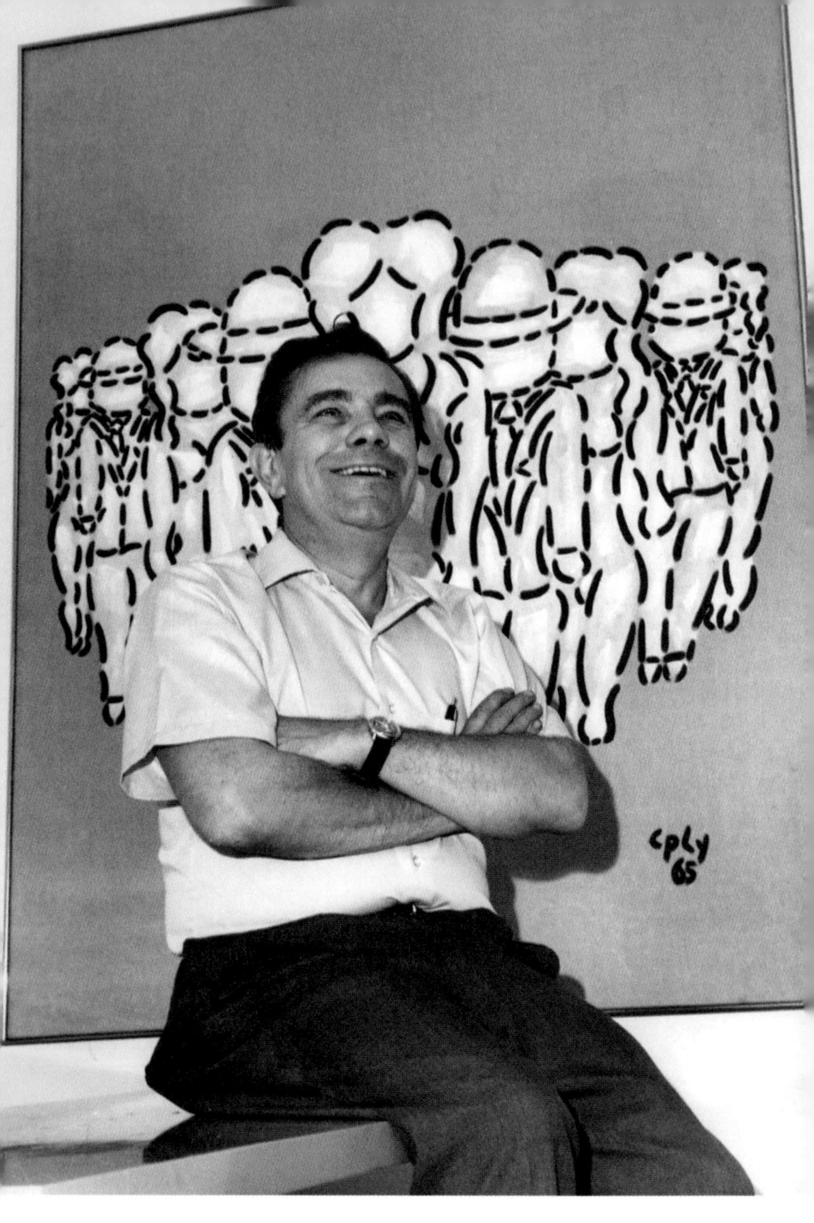

WILLIAM N. COPLEY

Der 1919 in New York City geborene Copley widmete sich ab 1947 ohne akademische Kunstausbildung der Malerei und lebte von 1951 bis 1962 in Paris. Dank seiner Tätigkeit als Journalist, Verleger, Galeriebesitzer und Kunstsammler war er eng vernetzt mit Künstlern wie Max Ernst, René Magritte, Marcel Duchamp und Man Ray. Viele seiner Arbeiten sind stark psychologisiert und weisen surreale Elemente auf. Auch seine Erfahrungen als Soldat im Zweiten Weltkrieg dürften ihre Spuren in seiner Kunst hinterlassen haben. Wie Iannone macht auch Copley sein eigenes Leben regelmäßig zum Gegenstand seiner Arbeit, schreibt bizarr humorvolle Memoiren und verbindet Bild- und Textelemente in surrealen Erzählstrukturen. In *The Evil I … Or The Story of My Life*, das teilweise an William Hogarth's *A Rakes Progress* angelehnt ist, fantasiert er seine eigene Lebensgeschichte, die seinen Fetischen eine Form gibt, ihn überspitzt als Millionär und Ehebrecher inmitten übergroßer Frauenfiguren zeigt, bevor ihn im letzten Bild seine Hinrichtung erwartet.

Copley, born in New York in 1919, focused on painting, for which he had no academic training, from 1947 onwards. From 1951 until 1962 he lived and worked in Paris. Through his activities as a journalist, publisher, gallerist, and art collector, he developed close ties with artists such as Max Ernst, René Magritte, Marcel Duchamp, and Man Ray. Many of his own works contain surreal elements and have a highly psychological basis. His experiences as a soldier in the Second World War may well also have influenced his art. Like Iannone, Copley too used his own life as a frequent subject for his work: he wrote bizarrely humorous memoirs, combining text

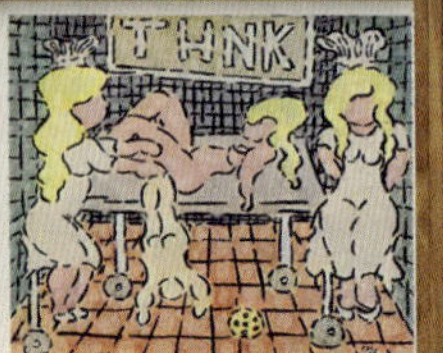

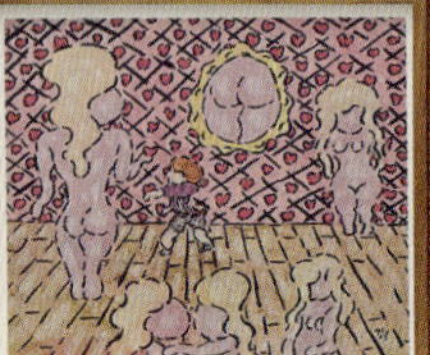
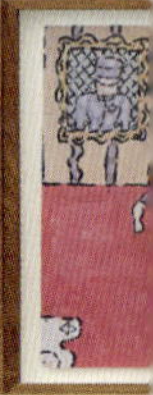

and visual imagery in surreal narrative structures. *The Evil I … Or The Story of My Life* creates a version of his own life, modelled partly on William Hogarth's *A Rakes Progress*, that gives shape to his fantasies and fetishes, and shows him in exaggerated form as a millionaire and adulterer among over-sized women, who ultimately awaits the guillotine.

Die Arbeiten in diesem Raum lassen sich wiederholende Bild-formeln erkennen: Frauen sind häufig übergroß und nackt, Männer tragen zu enge Anzüge und Melone oder berufsstän-dische Uniformen – Darstellungen, die in ihrer strikten Durch-formulierung und Überspitzung von Geschlechterrollen bis ins Absurde Copleys doppelbödigen Humor beweisen. Im Rückblick auf sein Gesamtwerk fällt auf, dass diese ironischen Motive ein Vokabular bilden, das Copley, den Regeln seiner eigenen Grammatik folgend, spielerisch zusammenfügt.

See Yourself as Lovers See You, der Titel der Ausstellung, ist zugleich Titel einer Malerei Copleys aus dem Jahr 1987. Der Satz erscheint außerdem in der dreiteiligen Publikation, die 1993 anlässlich der Ausstellung mit Dorothy Iannone und Emmett Williams entstand.

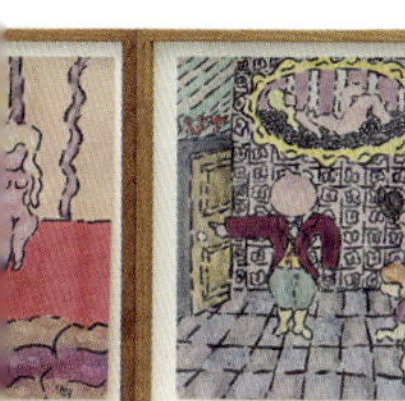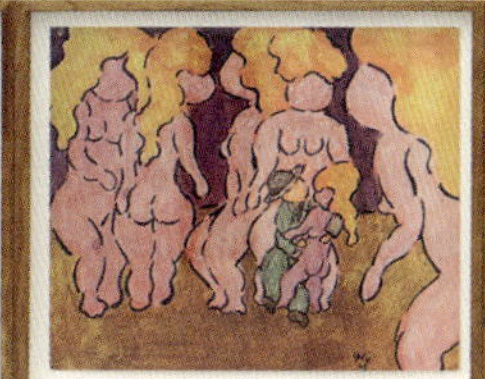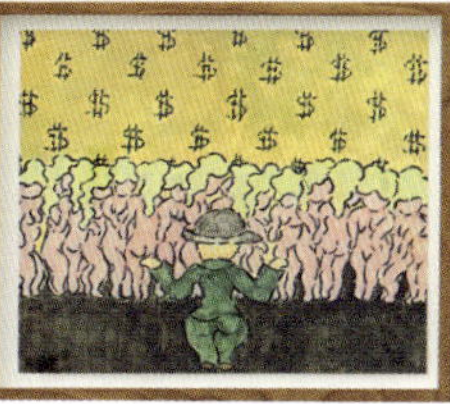

Several of Copley's recurrent images appear in the works in this room: in his pictures, women are often oversized and naked, men wear mandatory tight-fitting suits and bowler hats or professional uniforms. In their absolutely formulaic figuration and obsession with exaggeration of gender roles to the point of absurdity, they show an ambiguous humour. It is only on viewing his work as a whole that the irony of these motifs becomes clear, and they become the vocabulary for the idiosyncratic grammar that Copley uses in his playful approach.

See Yourself as Lovers See You is the title of both a 1987 painting by Copley and of this exhibition; the same words also appear in the pages of the three-part publication issued for the 1993 joint exhibition with Dorothy Iannone and Emmett Williams.

Auch *Dance of the Hours* war gemeinsam mit Werken Iannones in einer größeren Gruppenausstellung im Haus am Lützowplatz, Berlin, zu sehen. Das Tanzpaar, das den Bildraum dominiert, vermittelt im Zusammenspiel mit dem ornamentreichen Hintergrund einerseits unbeschwerte Ausgelassenheit, zugleich aber auch eine Spannung zwischen den Geschlechtern und wirft die Frage auf, wer das Tanzbein am höchsten schwingen kann.

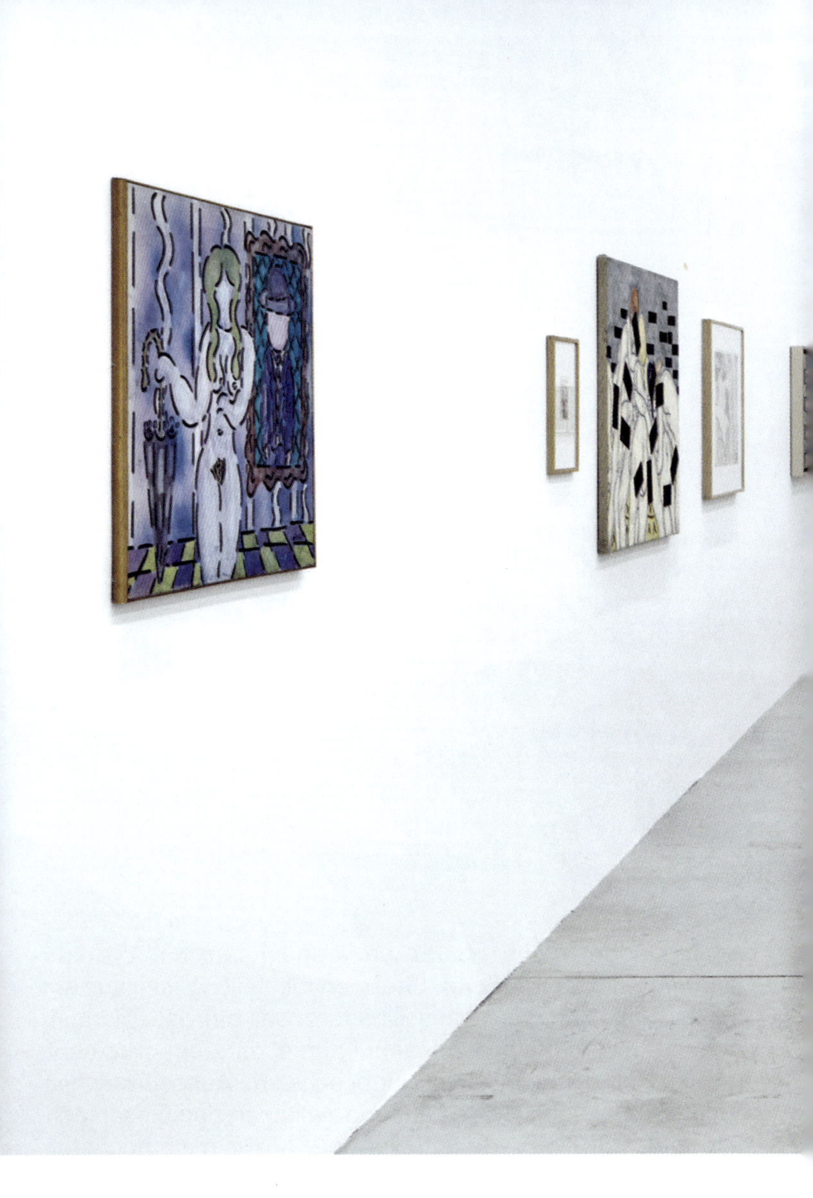

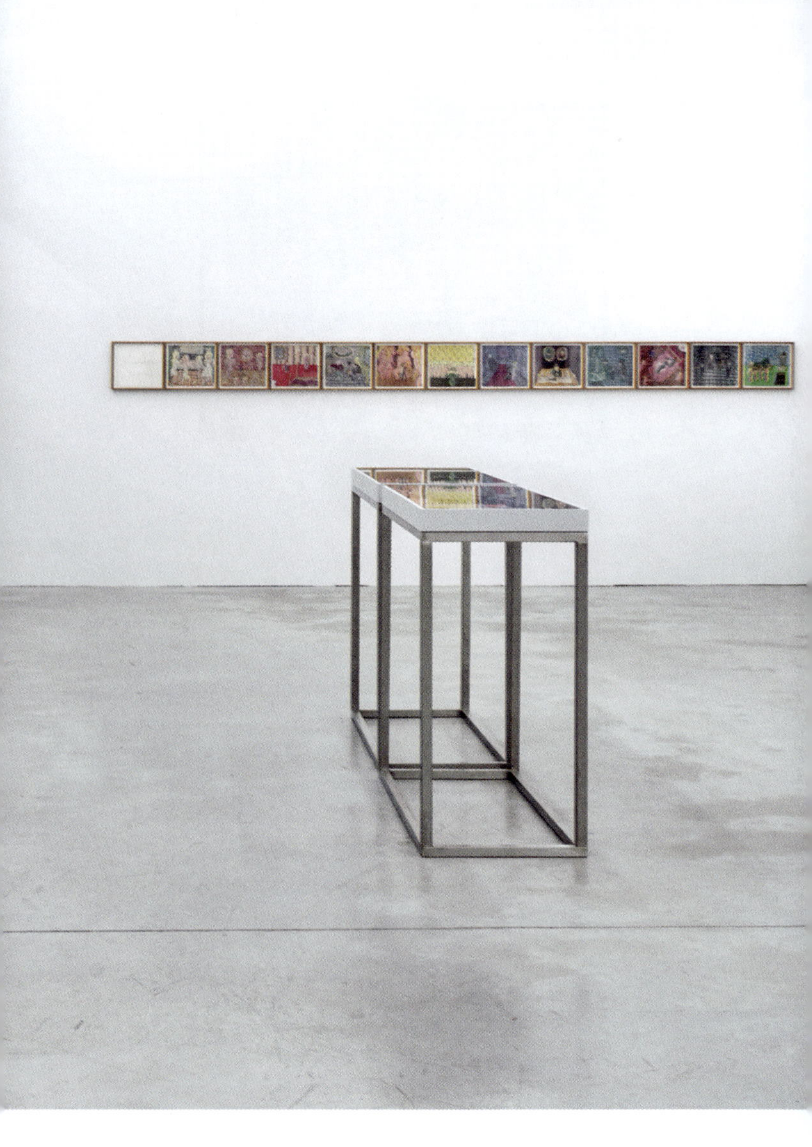

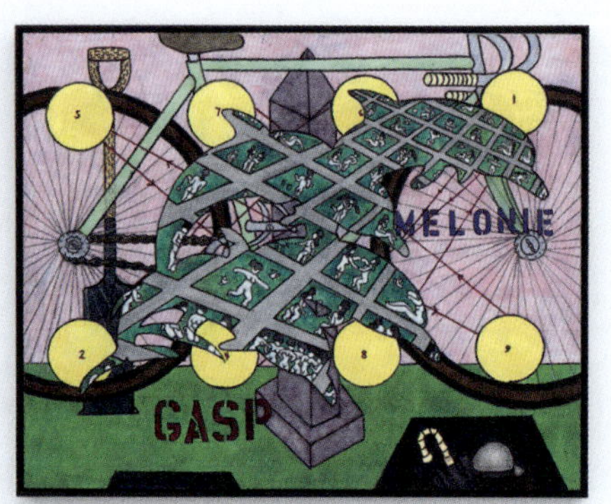
MELONIE
GASP

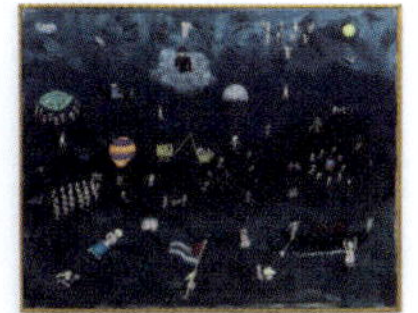 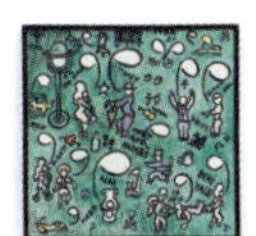 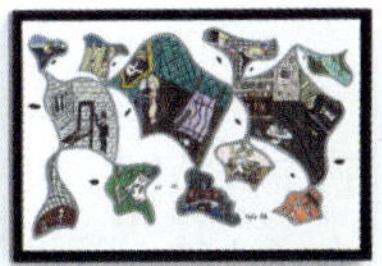

Dance of the Hours was shown in a larger group exhibition at the Haus am Lützowplatz, in which Iannone also participated. The dancing couple dominating the picture space, together with their richly ornamented background, convey both light-hearted exuberance and a competitive tension between the sexes over who can shake a leg the best on the dance floor.

Popkulturelle Bezüge stellte Copley auch durch Filmtitel her, die er zuweilen für seine Bilder verwendete, etwa bei *Towering Inferno*, das mehrere nackte Personen während einer Orgie zeigt. Die Arbeit wurde erst im Nachhinein vom Künstler mit schwarzen Zensurbalken übermalt und referenziert pornografische Magazine aus den 1960er und 1970er Jahren, in denen die Balken dazu dienten, die Identität von Personen zu verbergen. Möglicherweise inspiriert durch sein Werk *Eden* (1974), in dem er ebenfalls Zensurbalken verwendete, um die Identität der Figuren zu „schützen", nahm Copley zu einem späteren, unbekannten Zeitpunkt eine ironische Selbstzensur seines eigenen Bildes vor. Zudem fügte er im Hintergrund einen persönlichen, poetischen Text hinzu. Diese Änderungen verkomplizieren das Bild im Vergleich zu seinem früheren Stadium erheblich und stehen im Einklang mit Copleys Bestreben, „so viele Dimensionen wie möglich" – wie er es in den 1980er Jahren selbst formulierte – in seinen Bildern zu vereinen. Eine wichtige Rolle spielt die sexuelle Freiheit auch in seiner Serie *X-Rated*, die pornografische Magazine als Ausgangsmaterial nimmt und die Überschreitung und Infragestellung künstlerischer und sozialer Konventionen thematisiert. Anders als Iannone, deren Werke häufig zensiert wurden,[1] hatte Copley kaum mit Zensur zu kämpfen. Obgleich er oft damit rechnete, wurde selbst an seiner Ausstellung *X-Rated* kein Anstoß genommen. Lediglich eine Assemblage, die *Nous Deux* ähnelte und ebenso eine Spritze enthielt, musste er abhängen.

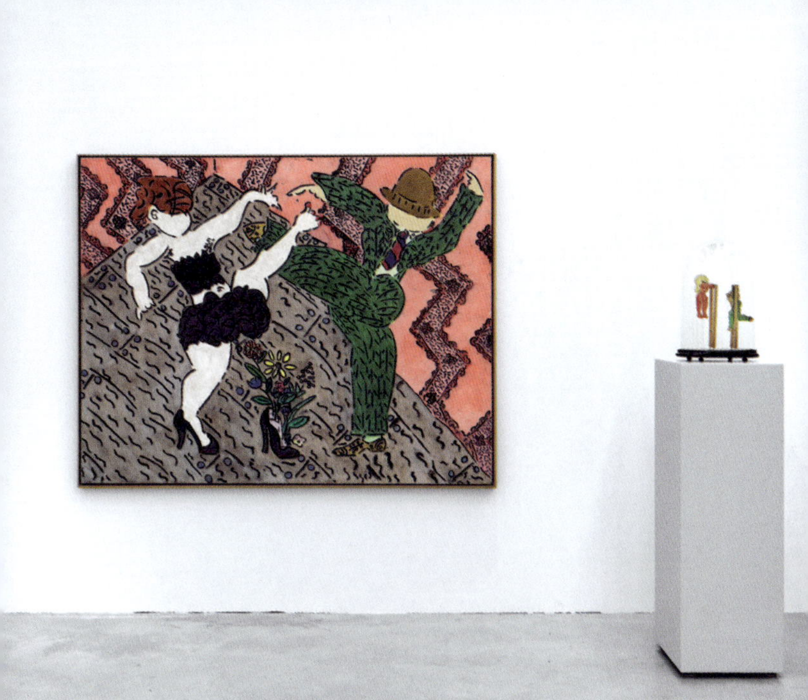

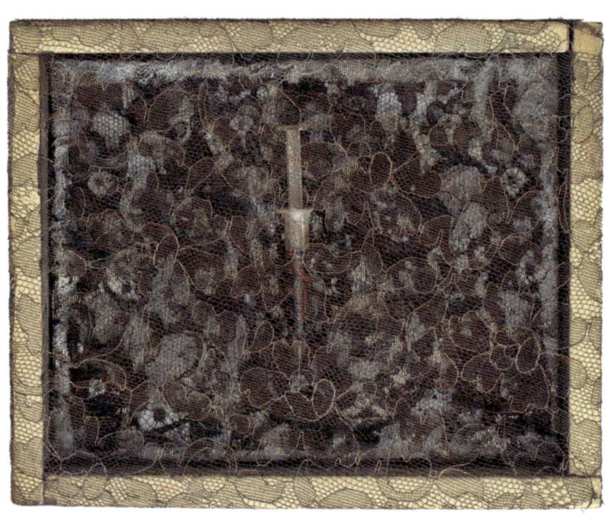

Copley also references pop culture in the film titles, such as *Towering Inferno*, that he sometimes uses for his pictures. This work depicts a group of naked people at an orgy; their naked bodies have been censored with several black bars, which the artist only added later, after the image was complete. This makes direct reference to the pornographic magazines of the 1960s and 1970s, in which black bars were used to conceal people's identities. Perhaps inspired by another of his pictures, *Eden* (1974), in which he used bars to 'hide' the identities of the figures, Copley decided at some unknown point to carry out ironic self-censorship on this work. He also added a poetic, personal text to the background of the picture. These later changes add considerable complexity in comparison with the earlier stage of the work, but are in accord with Copley's later aim, which he described in the late 1980s as the desire to round out his paintings with 'as many dimensions as possible'. Sexual freedom is also an important theme in Copley's *X-Rated* series, which uses pornographic magazines as source material and explores the joyous transgression and interrogation of artistic and social convention. Unlike Iannone, whose work was often censored,[2] Copley had to contend with relatively little censorship. Although he often expected it to happen to his work, even his *X-Rated* exhibition remained uncensored. Only when he used a hypodermic syringe in an assemblage similar his *Nous Deux* was Copley confronted with removal from view of his work.

Copley machte mit der Herausgabe seines innovativen Künstlermagazins *S.M.S.* zeitgenössische Kunst im kleinen Format zugänglich. In den insgesamt sechs im Abonnement erschienenen Ausgaben für jeweils 125 US-Dollar sind namenhafte Künstler*innen mit „originalen Reproduktionen" vertreten: So sind darin etwa ein laminiertes Papierschiffchen von Roy Lichtenstein, eine Lithografie von Meret Oppenheim, Klebstoff mit einer dazugehörigen Gebrauchsanweisung von Yoko Ono, nackte Anziehpuppen von Mel Ramos oder eine

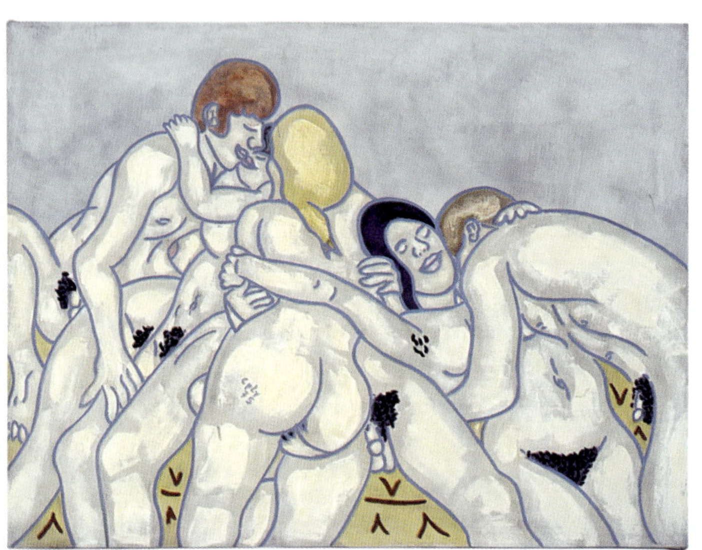

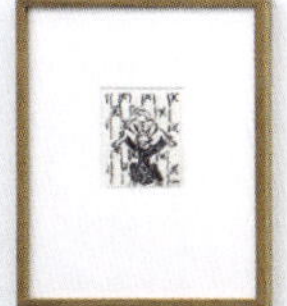

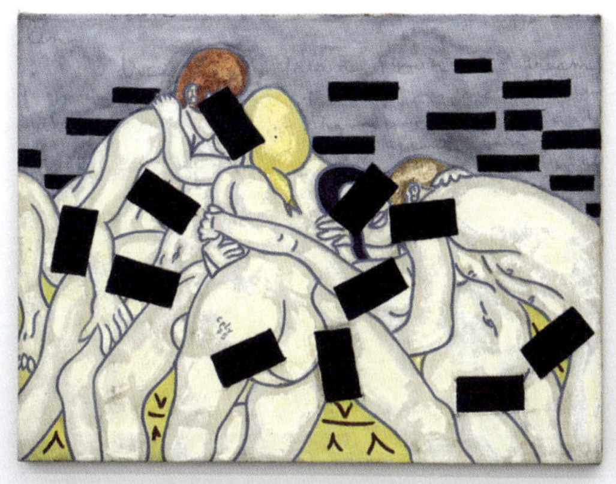

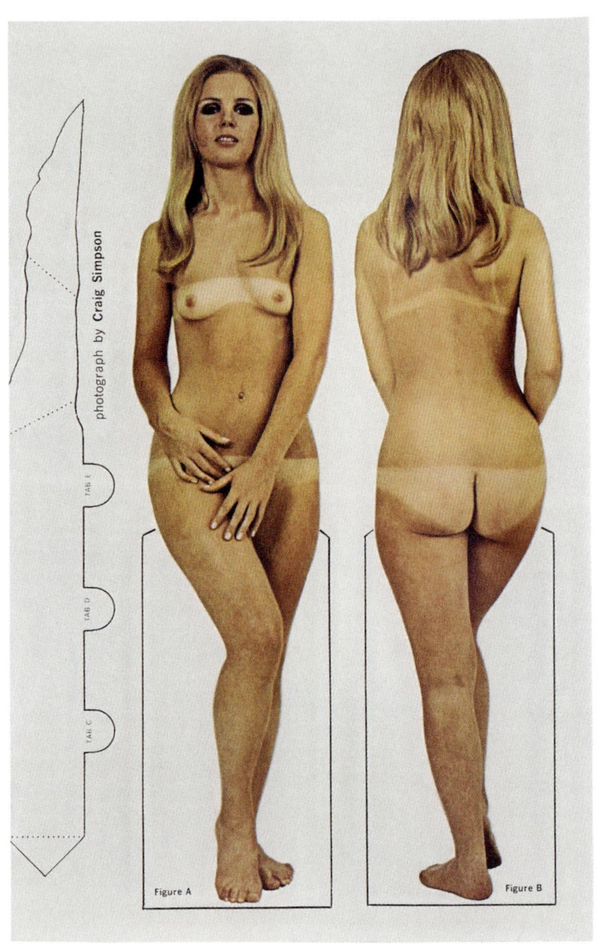
photograph by Craig Simpson
TAB E
TAB D
TAB C
Figure A
Figure B

Lithografie von Betty Dodson, einer Pionierin der Sexual-
aufklärung, zu finden. Die Publikationsreihe steht Zeuge dafür,
dass Copley es sich zur Aufgabe gemacht hatte, möglichst viel
unterschiedliche Ideen und überraschende Aspekte zu kombi-
nieren und seinem Publikum damit „erwachsene Freude" – so
seine Worte – zu bereiten.

Copley's publication of the innovative *S.M.S.* series of art edi-
tions made contemporary art accessible in small formats. In a
total of six issues, available by subscription for 125 US dollars
per issue, well-known artists were represented with 'original reproductions'. Subscribers would receive, for example,
a laminated paper boat by Roy Lichtenstein, a lithograph by
Meret Oppenheim, glue, with instructions for use, by Yoko Ono,
naked dress-up dolls by Mel Ramos, or a lithograph by Betty
Dodson, a pioneer of sexual enlightenment. They embody the
S.M.S. mission, which Copley declared was to convey surprising points of view and as many different ideas as possible,
thereby providing his subscribers with 'adult joy'.

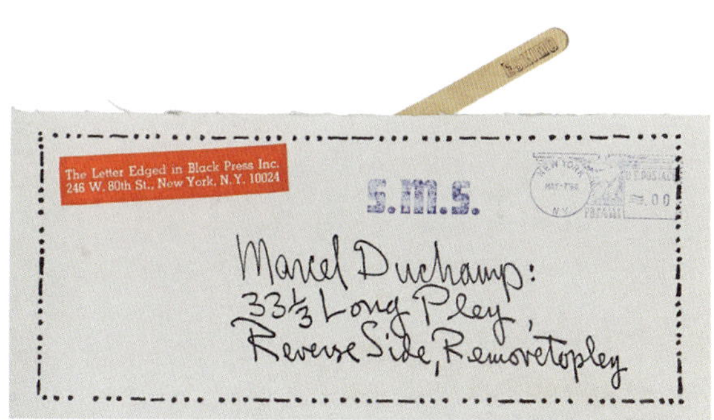

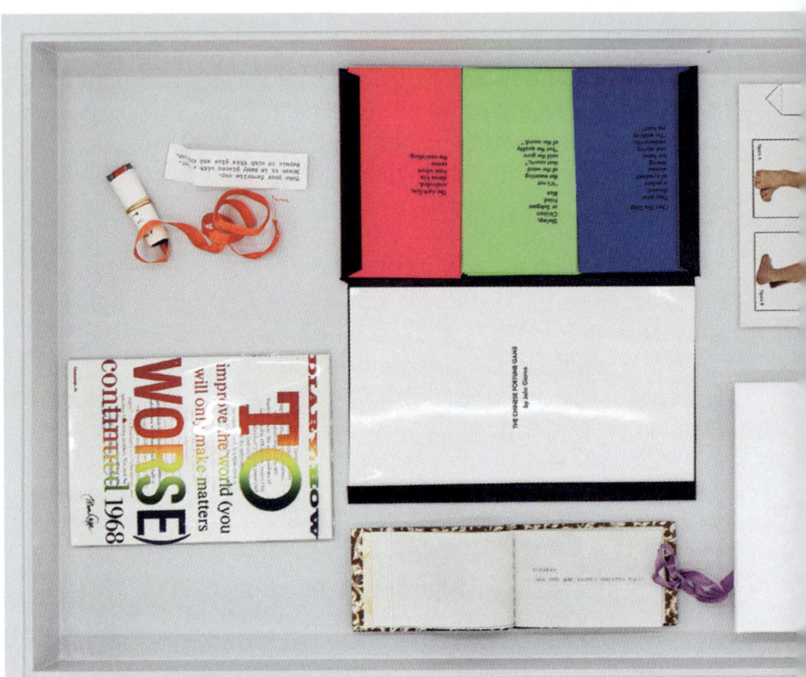

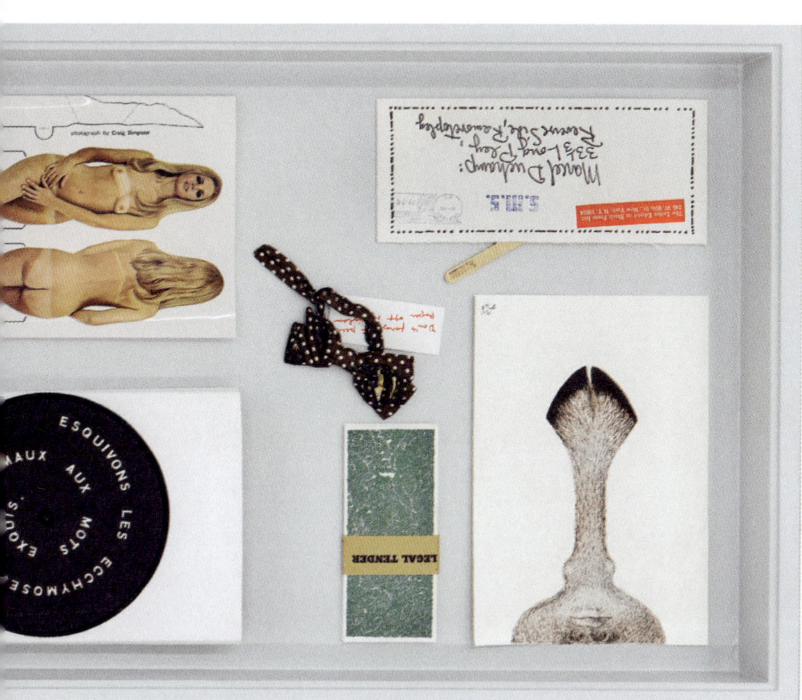
photograph by Craig Simpson
ESQUIVONS LES MOTS ECCHYMOSE EXOUIS. AUX MAUX
LEGAL TENDER
S.M.S.
Marcel Duchamp:
333 Long Road,
Reese Side, Ramenbefel
The Letter Edged in Black Press Inc.
246 W. 80th St., New York, N.Y. 10024
Don't forget the balloon

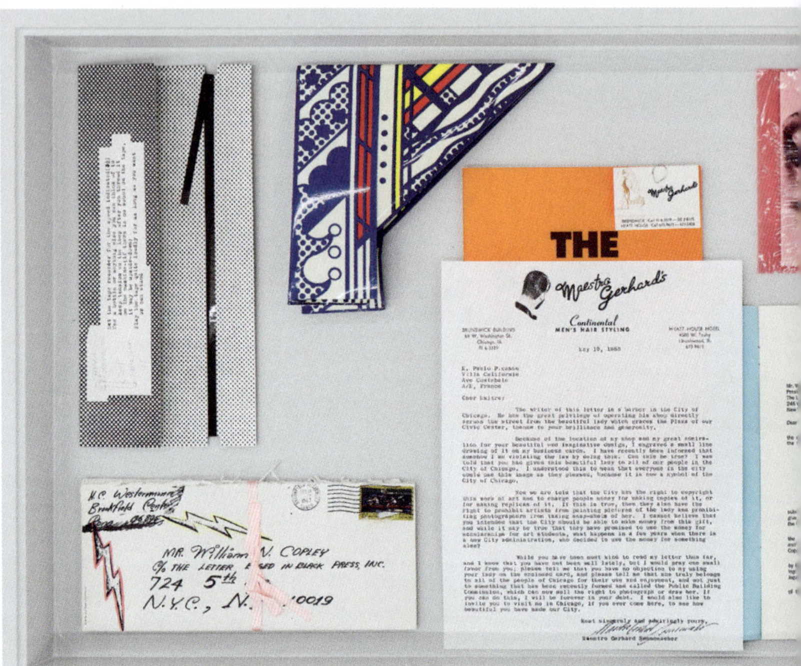

Maestro Gerhard's
Continental
MEN'S HAIR STYLING
BRUNSWICK BUILDING
69 W. Washington St.
Chicago, Il.
FI 6-1119
HYATT HOUSE HOTEL
4500 W. Touhy
Lincolnwood, Il.
673-9611
May 10, 1965

E. Pablo Picasso
Villa California
Ave Costebele
A/M, France

Cher Maitre:

The writer of this letter is a barber in the City of Chicago. He has the great privilege of operating his shop directly across the street from the beautiful lady which graces the Plaza of our Civic Center, thanks to your brilliance and generosity.

Because of the location of my shop and my great admiration for your beautiful and imaginative design, I engraved a small line drawing of it on my business cards. I have recently been informed that somehow I am violating the law by doing this. Can this be true? I was told that you had given this beautiful lady to all of our people in the City of Chicago. I understood this to mean that everyone in the city could use this image as they pleased, because it is now a symbol of the City of Chicago.

Now we are told that the City has the right to copyright this work of art and to charge people money for making copies of it, or for making replicas of it. If this is true, then they also have the right to prohibit artists from painting pictures of the lady and prohibiting photographers from taking snap-shots of her. I cannot believe that you intended that the City should be able to make money from this gift, and while it may be true that they have promised to use the money for scholarships for art students, what happens in a few years when there is a new City administration, who decided to use the money for something else?

While you have been most kind to read my letter thus far, and I know that you have not been well lately, but I would pray one small favor from you; please tell me that you have no objection to my using your lady on the enclosed card, and please tell me that she truly belongs to all of the people of Chicago for their use and enjoyment, and not just to something that has been recently formed and called the Public Building Commission, which can now sell the right to photograph or draw her. If you can do this, I will be forever in your debt. I would also like to invite you to visit me in Chicago, if you ever come here, to see how beautiful you have made our City.

Most sincerely and admiringly yours,

Maestro Gerhard Schomacher

THE

M.C. Westermann
Brookfield Center
Conn. 06805

MR. William N. Copley
C/o THE LETTER EDGED IN BLACK PRESS, INC.
724 5th
N.Y.C., N.   10019

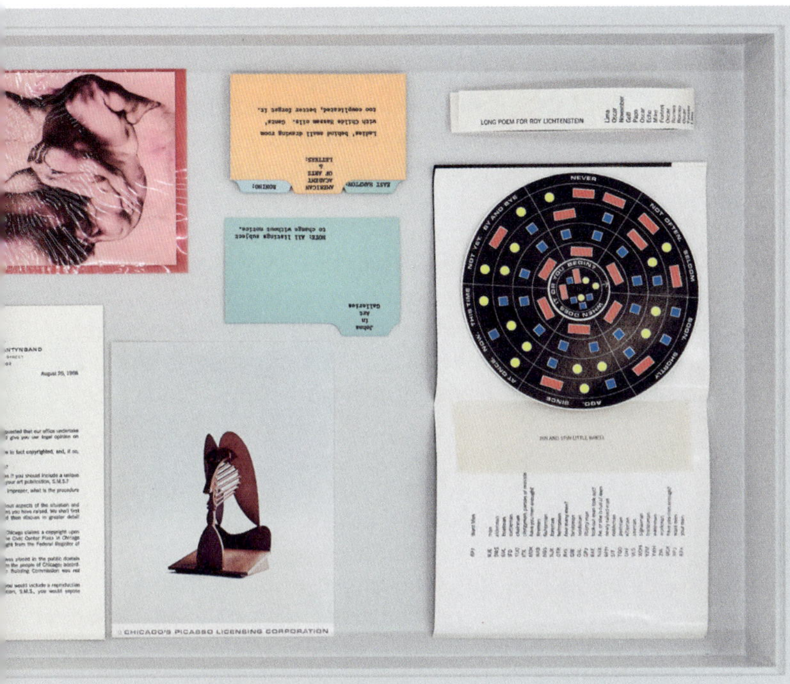

LONG POEM FOR ROY LICHTENSTEIN
NEVER
NOT OFTEN SELDOM
SOON
SHORTLY
ADD.
SINCE
AT ONCE NOW
THIS TIME
BY AND BYE
NOT YET
WHEN DOES IT OR YOU BEGIN?
SPIN AND SPIN LITTLE WHEEL
© CHICAGO'S PICASSO LICENSING CORPORATION

In Anlehnung an die Ausstellung haben wir eine kleine Hör- und Lese-Lounge mit Büchern und Schallplatte eingerichtet. Ein Schuber der Ausstellung im Haus am Lützowplatz (1993) zeigt die Publikationen von Copley und Iannone, in denen auch der Titel der Ausstellung, *See Yourself as Lovers See You,* enthalten ist. Des Weiteren ist hier die 2015 produzierte Schallplatte *Ewig Grün* von Iannone zu finden. Darauf zu hören ist eine Audioaufnahme aus dem Jahr 1975, in der die Künstlerin einen Ausschnitt aus einem deutschen Volkslied singt. Aus Freude über ein Stipendium in Berlin startete die Künstlerin eine Aufnahme mit dem Kassettenrecorder, in der sie denselben Satz mehrfach wiederholt, während sie sich selbst befriedigt.

Linked to the exhibition, we have set up a small audio and reading lounge, with a record and books. A slipcase from the 1993 exhibition at the Haus am Lützowplatz, containing the publications on Copley and Iannone, in which are the words of the exhibition title, *See Yourself as Lovers See You,* can be seen here. Here too is *Ewig Grün*, a record, produced in 2015, of Iannone singing a German popular song, which she originally taped on a cassette recorder in 1975, then reproduced on vinyl during her time in Berlin. On this record, the artist is heard singing the same sentences over and over while she pleasures herself.

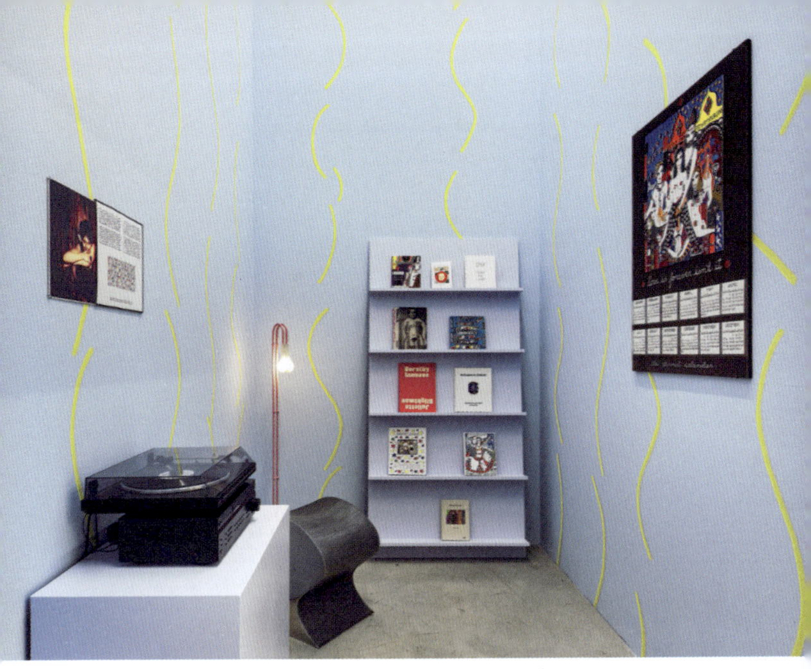

1   Ein gutes Beispiel hierfür ist die Zensur ihrer Ausstellung bei Harald Szeemann in der Kunsthalle Bern, die danach nach Düsseldorf reiste. Iannone publizierte ein Künstlerinnenbuch über ihre Erfahrung: Dorothy Iannone: The Story of Bern, [or] Showing Colors (1970).

2   A striking example is the censorship of her exhibition with Harald Szeemann at the Kunsthalle Bern, which afterwards travelled to Düsseldorf. Iannone published an artist's book about this experience: Dorothy Iannone, The Story of Bern, [or] Showing Colors (1970).

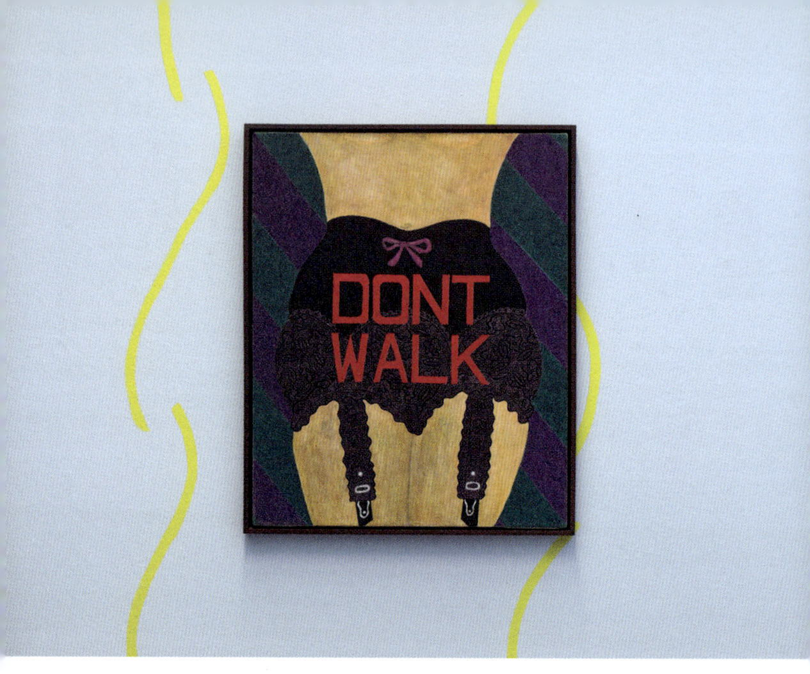

DONT
WALK

SEE YOURSELF AS LOVERS SEE YOU

Ein Gespräch mit Florence Bonnefous vom Dorothy Iannone Estate und Anthony Atlas vom William N. Copley Estate

A conversation with Florence Bonnefous of the Dorothy Iannone Estate and Anthony Atlas of the William N. Copley Estate

Julika Bosch (JB): Wer sich mit dem Leben von William N. Copley und Dorothy Iannone vertraut macht, entdeckt trotz aller Unterschiede viele interessante Parallelen, sowohl biografisch als auch in ihren Werken. Beide studierten Sprache und Linguistik – William N. Copley Englisch, Dorothy Iannone amerikanische und englische Literatur – und nicht etwa Kunst, bevor sie mit der Malerei begannen. Wie schlägt sich das in ihren Werken nieder?

Florence Bonnefous (FB): Tatsächlich war Literatur als Kunst- und Ausdrucksform für Dorothy immer von großer Bedeutung, und auch in ihren visuellen Arbeiten griff sie das Thema ganz bewusst auf. Zwar begann sie das Malen 1959 in einem ziemlich rohen Stil des abstrakten Expressionismus, aber schon 1962 erscheinen Wörter oder Textcollagen auf ihren Bildern. Das Schreiben war immer Teil ihrer künstlerischen Praxis. Außerdem pflegte sie langjährige Briefwechsel mit Freund*innen, vor allem aus den USA, Frankreich und Deutschland. Diesen regen Schriftverkehr verstaute sie sorgfältig in Schuhkartons. Er begleitete sie während ihrer gesamten Zeit im Ausland von einem Ort zum nächsten. Die Briefe beziehen sich, genau wie sämtliche ihrer Werke, sehr oft auf literarische Schriften. Das Künstlerinnenbuch war für Dorothy ein wichtiges stilistisches Mittel und wurde zum festen Bestandteil ihres Schaffens. Ich plane, sämtliche dieser Bücher der Berlinischen Galerie zu übergeben, genauso wie einen Großteil ihrer Korrespondenz. Andere Teile ihrer schriftstellerischen Arbeit gehen an verschiedene französische und amerikanische Museen.

Anthony Atlas (AA): Copley machte nie einen offiziellen College-Abschluss, weil er Yale zu Beginn seines dritten Studienjahres verließ, um im Zweiten Weltkrieg zu dienen. Aber er studierte dort Englisch und betrachtete sich selbst als Schriftsteller, bevor er in den späten 1940er Jahren zur Kunst kam. Er liebte das Werk von James Joyce und begann ursprünglich mit der Malerei, um seine „visuelle Wahrnehmung" zu schärfen, wie er selbst sagte. Er war der Meinung, dass sich seine Schreibe dadurch verbessern würde.[1] Nachdem er das Malen einmal angefangen hatte, hörte er nie wieder damit auf. In einem Interview von 1976 sagte Copley: „Meine Gemälde sind beinahe literarische Aussagen [...] genauso wie ein Gedicht eine Aussage ist."[2] Die literarische Dimension spielte also auch bei ihm eine große Rolle. Sie lieferte ein Analogon für das, was Copley mit seinem eigenen Werk erreichen wollte, und in manchen Fällen auch das direkte Quellenmaterial.

JB: Getting acquainted with both the lives of William N. Copley and Dorothy Iannone, it is interestingly easy to notice many parallels in both their lives and their works (while also acknowledging their differences, of course). They both studied for degrees in language/linguistics-related subjects – William N. Copley in English and Dorothy Iannone in American and English Literature – not in art, before they approached painting. In what ways did this influence their work?

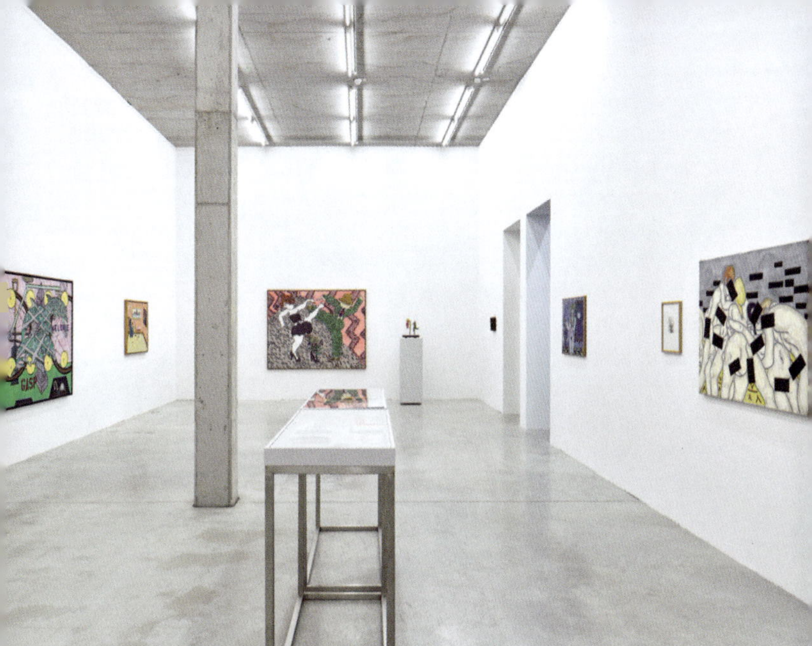

FB: Indeed, literature as a form of art and expression was always of major importance to Dorothy, and it became a very conscious part of her visual artworks as well. Although she began painting in 1959 with rather brutal abstract expressionism, words or collages of pages of text appear in these works as early as 1962. A lot of writing accompanied her practice. In addition, she developed long-term correspondence with friends, mainly in the USA, France and Germany. This abundant correspondence was carefully preserved, stored in shoeboxes, and accompanied her from one place to another throughout her expatriate life. These letters very often refer to literary writings, as indeed do all her works. The artist's book became her regular mode of expression. I plan to place all her artist's books with the Berlinische Galerie, as well as a large part of her correspondence, while other batches will be distributed to various French and American museums.

AA: Copley never actually received an official college degree, because he left Yale early in his third year to serve in World War Two. But Copley did study English at Yale and considered himself a writer before he became an artist in the late 1940s. He loved the work of James Joyce and originally started painting, as he said, to sharpen his 'visual perception', which he thought would improve his writing.[3] But once he started painting, he never stopped. In a 1976 interview, Copley said 'My paintings are almost literary statements […] like a poem is a statement.'[4] So the literary dimension was a huge influence for him, too – it provided an analogue for what Copley aspired to do with his own work and, in some cases, direct source material as well.

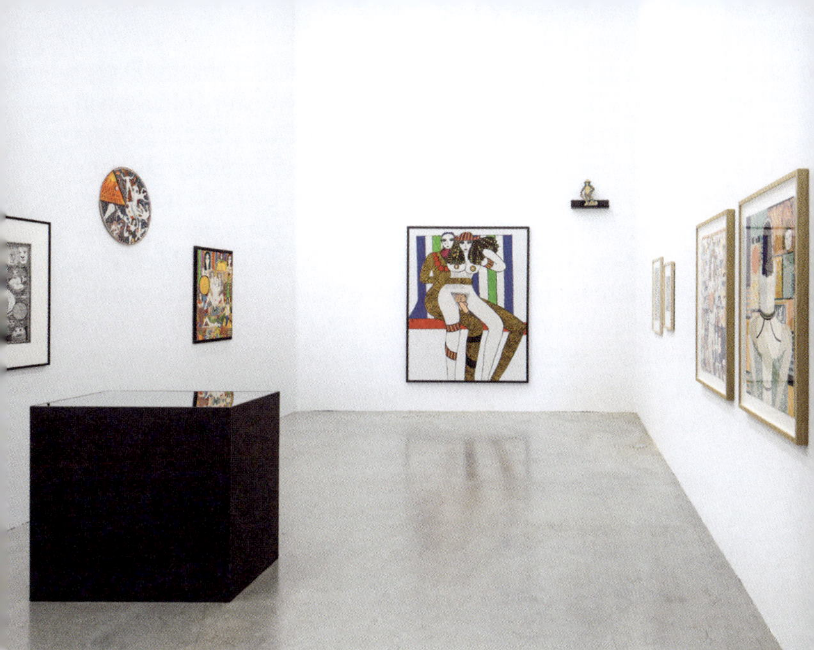

JB: Beide gelten als autodidaktische Künstler*innen. Diese Formulierung könnte jetzt den Eindruck erwecken, dass sie in der Kunstszene Außenseiter*innen waren. Das trifft auf Copley und Iannone aber nicht zu: Von 1963 bis 1967 betrieb Dorothy Iannone zusammen mit ihrem Mann James Upham, der Maler war, die *The Stryke Gallery*. Dort stellten sie eigene Werke und die anderer Künstler*innen aus. Copley, der Man Ray und Marcel Duchamp nahestand, eröffnete 1948/49 zusammen mit dem Künstler John Ployardt die *Copley Galleries*, wo Werke von Joseph Cornell, Max Ernst, René Magritte, Roberto Matta, Man Ray und Yves Tanguy gezeigt wurden. Wie wurden die beiden Neuankömmlinge in der Szene aufgenommen?

AA: Copley und Ployardt hatten übergroße Ambitionen, als sie ihre Galerie, die 1948 eröffnet wurde, Ende 1947 gemeinsam gründeten. Ployardt war Zeichner für Disney und selbst ein talentierter Künstler, aber nicht wirklich bekannt. Die beiden Männer hatten sich über ihre Ehefrauen, die Schwestern Lila und Doris Wead, kennengelernt. Ployardt war 31, Copley 28. Ployardt führte Copley an den Surrealismus heran, und das beeinflusste letzteren ganz maßgeblich. Über ihr erstes Treffen mit Man Ray schrieb Copley später: „Ich glaube, er war berührt von unserer Jugend, unserem Aberwitz und unserer Bewunderung für ihn."[5] Im Frühjahr 1948, nach Ployardts und Copleys erstem Besuch in Sedona, schrieb Dorothea Tanning an Joseph Cornell, sie sei ganz bezaubert von den „netten Jungs aus Hollywood" und wünsche ihnen Erfolg.[6] Sicher waren sie Neulinge, aber sehr gewinnende. Später betonte Copley oft, wie wichtig es sei, bei denjenigen, die er bewunderte, „an die Türen zu klopfen", und dass die meisten Künstler*innen anderen das Interesse an ihrer Arbeit „nicht übelnehmen" würden.[7] Diese Einstellung machte die *Copley Galleries* möglich.

FB: Ich habe mit Dorothy kaum über diese frühen Jahre gesprochen, da wir viel mit der Gegenwart zu tun hatten. Aber zweifellos war sie eine dieser abenteuerlichen, impulsiven Freigeister, denen egal ist, was die Leute denken. Lustigerweise organisierte ich (bei Esther Schipper in Berlin) eine Ausstellung, die Dorothy mit Lily van der Stokker zusammenbrachte, einer Künstlerin, die auch am Anfang ihrer Karriere stand – sie hatte gerade eine eigene Galerie in New York eröffnet – und ebenfalls Worte in ihre Muster einbaute.

JB: They are both considered self-taught artists, but these terms often come with the assumption that they were outsiders on the art scene, which for Copley and Iannone wasn't the case: From 1963 to 1967 Dorothy Iannone ran a gallery called *The Stryke Gallery* together with her husband James Upham, who was a painter, where they exhibited their own work as well as that of other artists. And in 1948–1949 Copley, who was close to Man Ray and Marcel Duchamp, opened the Copley Galleries together with the artist John Ployardt, showcasing works by Joseph Cornell, Max Ernst, René Magritte, Roberto Matta, Man Ray, and Yves Tanguy. What can you tell us about the way they were perceived in the scene when they entered?

AA: Copley and Ployardt had outsized ambition when they co-founded the gallery in late 1947 (opening to the public in autumn 1948). Ployardt was an animator for Disney and a talented artist in his own right, but not well known. The two men met through their respective wives, Lila and Doris Wead, who were sisters. Ployardt was 31, Copley was 28. Ployardt introduced Copley to Surrealism, and this had a massive impact on him. Copley later wrote about their first meeting with Man Ray: 'I think he was touched by our youth and lunacy and our homage.'[8] Dorothea Tanning, writing to Joseph Cornell in spring

1948, was charmed by these 'nice lads from Hollywood' after their first visit to Sedona, and wished them success.[9] They were definitely newcomers, but endearing too. Later, Copley would often stress the importance of 'knocking on the doors' of those he admired, saying 'most artists don't resent others' interest in their work.[10] This attitude made the Copley Galleries possible.

FB: I hardly talked with Dorothy about those early years, as we had much to do together with the present, but she was certainly one of those adventurous, impulsive free spirits who don't care what people think. Funnily enough, I organised an exhibition (at Esther Schipper in Berlin) that brought together Dorothy Iannone and Lily van der Stokker, who also began her career as an artist by opening her own gallery in New York and includes words in her patterns.

JB: Während sie ihren jeweils eigenen Stil ausbildeten, lösten sich Copley und Iannone behutsam vom Mainstream: Beide hatten rein gar nichts mit der minimalistischen Kunstbewegung am Hut, und beide verwendeten popkulturelle Referenzen in ihren Werken, können aber trotzdem nicht der Pop Art zuge- rechnet werden. Auch aus anderen Bewegungen fallen sie eher heraus. Copley war umgeben von Surrealist*innen und Dadaist*innen und bediente sich in seinem Symbolismus klar ihrer visuellen Motive – die Melone, der Regenschirm, das Schachbrett –, aber seine Bildsprache unterscheidet sich von der ihren. Auch kunstgeschichtlich betrachtet war er zu spät dran, als dass man ihn einer dieser Strömungen zuordnen könnte.

Dorothy Iannone orientierte sich in ihrem frühen Werk am abstrakten Expressionismus, von dem sie sich jedoch schnell wieder abwandte, um ihrem eigenen, figurativeren Stil zu fol- gen. Später galt sie als Mitglied der Fluxus-Bewegung. In einer Aufnahme von 1979 allerdings sagt sie: „Ich bin diejenige, die Fluxus-Künstlerin ist, die keine Fluxus-Künstlerin ist."[11]

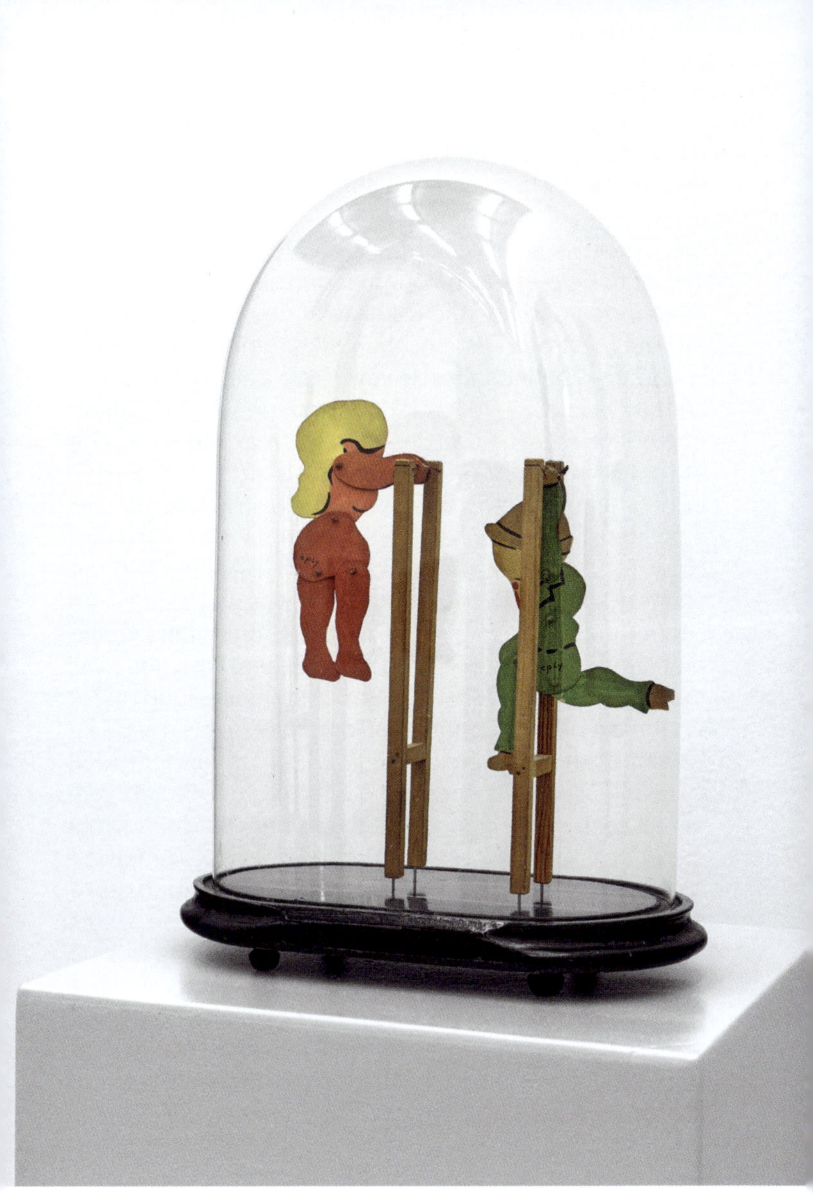

Was könnt ihr uns über Iannones und Copleys Meinung zu Kategorisierungen in der Kunstwelt, zum „engen Korsett der Ismen", sagen? Welche Rolle spielt ihre (teilweise strikte) Verweigerung, sich in eine Schublade stecken zu lassen, in der (historischen) Wahrnehmung ihrer Arbeit?

AA: Der inzwischen verstorbene Kurator Germano Celant erkannte Copleys Abneigung gegen stilistische Kategorisierungen und hob die Radikalität des Künstler hervor, der die Welt des Persönlichen erkundete, während viele andere Kunstschaffende vom Ende des Zweiten Weltkriegs bis in die 1960er Jahre hinein unter dem Zauber des Action Painting und des abstrakten Expressionismus standen.[12] Was Pop Art angeht, bildete sich Copleys Bildsprache während der 1950er Jahre in Frankreich heraus, abseits von den Zentren der Szene in London und New York. Als er Ende 1962 in die USA zurückkehrte und nach New York zog, hatte die Bewegung bereits ihre Stars, und Copleys eigenwilliger Figurativismus wollte nicht recht in die Pop-Schablone passen. Trotzdem wurde er in mehrere bekannte Pop-Art-Ausstellungen der ersten Stunde aufgenommen, darunter *Pop Art USA* im Oakland Art Museum im Jahr 1963, kuratiert von John Coplans. Auch in seiner Serie *Flags* von 1961–62, die ich zu seinen wichtigen Arbeiten zählen würde, obwohl sie eher unbekannt ist, wandte er viele der Bildstrategien aus der Pop Art an. Wäre Copley gezwungen gewesen, einen „Ismus" für sich zu wählen, hätte er sich wohl als Surrealist identifiziert, vor allem wegen des Einflusses, den die Mitglieder der Szene auf ihn als Person hatten. „Ich nenne mich nur einen Surrealisten wegen meiner Verbindung zu den Menschen", hat er einmal gesagt, „und weil ich mir mit ihnen einig bin. Bei ihnen bin ich zu Hause."[13]

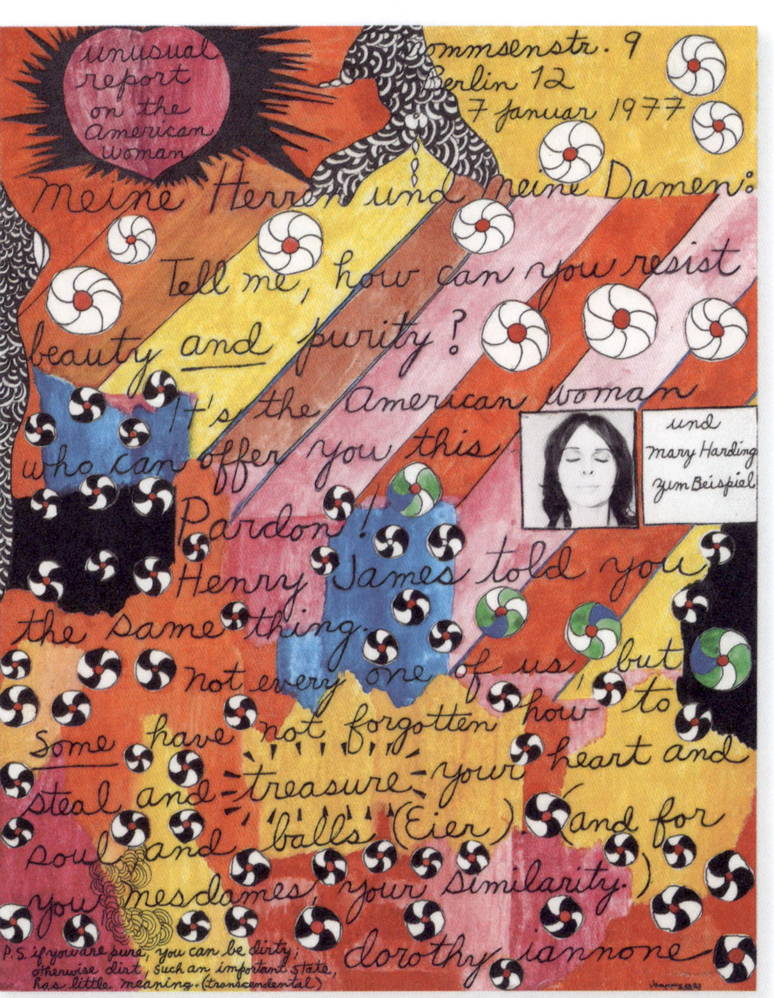

unusual report on the American Woman

Tommsenstr. 9
Berlin 12
7 Januar 1977

Meine Herren und Meine Damen:

Tell me, how can you resist beauty and purity? It's the American Woman who can offer you this Pardon! Henry James told you the same thing. Not every one of us, but some have not forgotten how to steal and treasure your heart and soul and 'balls' (Eier). (and for you mesdames, your similarity.)

und
Mary Harding
zum Beispiel

dorothy iannone

P.S. if you are pure, you can be dirty; otherwise dirt, such an important state, has little meaning. (transcendental)

FB: Dorothy hätte kein solches Statement zu irgendwelchen Zugehörigkeiten abgegeben. Sie war eine freiheitsliebende Frau, die sich gegen Kategorisierungen stemmte. Als eine Art inspirierte Abenteurerin durchstreifte sie verschiedene gesellschaftliche und künstlerische Gruppen, knüpfte und pflegte dabei aber während ihres gesamten Lebens auch bemerkenswert enge Freundschaften.

JB: When they each established their individual styles, both Copley and Iannone gently broke away from the mainstream: while both were extremely far removed from the Minimalist art movement, they also used Pop references in their works, but cannot be part of what is now considered true Pop Art. They also seem to fall outside other movements. Copley was surrounded by Surrealists and Dadaists, and clearly referenced their visual motifs – the bowler hat, the umbrella, the chess board – in his symbolism, but his visual language differs from these movements and, when viewed through the lens of art history, is considered too late to be part of them.

Dorothy Iannone was influenced in her early years by Abstract Expressionism, which she quickly moved away from, diverting into a more figurative style, and she was later received as a member of the Fluxus movement. However, in *A Fluxus Essay (2016). Whenever one wants to put them in the tight corset of Isms, they clearly refuse…* , she states, for example, that: 'I am she who is the Fluxus woman artist who is not the Fluxus woman artist.'[14]

What can you tell us about their perception in terms of the narrow corsets of art Isms? What part does their (sometimes outright) refusal to be categorised in that manner play in the (historical) perception of their work?

AA: The late curator Germano Celant was perceptive about Copley's stylistic refusals, highlighting the radicality of this artist who explored the personal realm, while so many other artists – between the end of World War Two and the 1960s – were under the spell of Action Painting and Abstract Expressionism.[15] With regard to Pop Art, Copley's visual language had developed in France in the 1950s, relatively separate from the scenes in London and New York, where the movement developed. By the time he returned to the USA, moving to New York at the end of 1962, Pop had already found its stars, and Copley's idiosyncratic figural mode would not fit neatly into its rubric. Nevertheless, Copley was included in several landmark early Pop Art surveys, including *Pop Art USA* (curated by John Coplans) at the Oakland Art Museum in 1963. There is also Copley's *Flags* series from 1961–62, which could be considered an important, but relatively lesser-known body of work that employed many of the pictorial strategies associated with Pop Art.

But if pressed to choose an 'ism' of his own, Copley would identify himself as a Surrealist, mostly for the personal influence these artists had on him. 'I only call myself a Surrealist simply because of my association with the people themselves,' he said, 'and the fact that I agree with those people, I am at home with them.'[16]

FB: Dorothy, on the other hand, wouldn't have made a statement of association of this kind: she was a free thinker, resistant to categorisation. A kind of inspired adventurer, she moved in diverse social and artistic groups, but also developed and maintained singularly strong friendships throughout her life.

JB: Genau, zum Beispiel zu Emmett Williams. Er war eng mit Iannone befreundet und stellte 1993 gemeinsam mit ihr und Copley aus. Da Williams' Bildsprache sich deutlicher von denen der anderen beiden unterscheidet, haben wir uns für unsere Ausstellung in der Sammlung Philara entschieden, den Schwerpunkt auf Iannone und Copley zu legen. Aber Williams war für Iannone von großer Bedeutung, richtig?

FB: Ja, Emmett Williams war ein guter Freund von Dorothy und eine Schlüsselfigur in ihrem Leben. Er begleitete Dorothy und James auf ihre Reisen durch Europa, insbesondere nach Island im Juni 1967, wo sie ihre „Muse" Dieter Roth traf, aber auch nach Südfrankreich, zum Cap d'Antibes (Dorothy kehrte nach ihrer Trennung von Dieter Roth dorthin zurück und lebte in Saint Jeannet), wo sie Robert und Marcelline Filliou kennenlernte, die ihre engsten Freund*innen werden sollten. Robert würdigte Dorothys vollkommene humanistische Freiheit: „Sie ist eine Freiheitskämpferin und eine kraftvolle und leidenschaftliche Künstlerin, die Bild und Text, Schönheit und Wahrheit geschickt miteinander verbindet. Ihr Ziel ist nicht weniger als die Befreiung der Menschheit." Dorothy traf sich persönlich und schrieb Briefe mit ihnen, ebenso mit George Brecht, mit dem sie eine gemeinsame Möbelreihe plante.

JB: Yes, for example Emmett Williams. He was a close friend of Iannone and exhibited alongside both Iannone and Copley in 1993. As Williams' visual language differs more obviously from each of their respective styles, we chose to focus on Iannone and Copley in our exhibition at the Philara Collection. Though I would consider him especially important for Iannone, right?

FB: Yes, Emmett Williams was a close friend of Dorothy's, and indeed a key figure in her life. It was he who accompanied Dorothy and James on their European travels, in particular to Iceland in June 1967, where she met her 'muse', Dieter Roth, but also to the South of France, to Cap d'Antibes (she returned there after her separation from Dieter Roth, and lived in Saint Jeannet), where she met Robert and Marcelline Filliou, who were to become her best friends. Robert paid tribute to Dorothy's absolute humanist freedom thus: 'She is a freedom fighter, and a forceful and dedicated artist, skilfully blending imagery and text, beauty and truth. Her aim is no less than human liberation.' She met and corresponded with them, as well as with George Brecht, with whom she planned a furniture edition.

JB: In welcher Weise stand Copley mit Emmett Williams in Verbindung, Anthony?

AA: In den späten 1960er Jahren erhielt Williams ein Stipendium für bildende Künste von Copleys wohltätiger Stiftung, der Cassandra Foundation (ursprünglich William and Noma Copley Foundation). Die freundschaftliche Beziehung entstand wahrscheinlich über Dieter Roth, der auch Iannones Beitrag (*LBJ*, 1968) zur nicht realisierten siebten Ausgabe von Copleys Magazin *S.M.S.* angeregt hatte. Die eben erwähnte Ausstellung *Berliner Amerikaner* von 1993 zeigte Williams, Copley und Dorothy Iannone Seite an Seite, wobei Copley, wie ich vermute, eher als geladener Gast dabei war, denn er war zwar Amerikaner, lebte aber nicht in Berlin, sondern auf den Florida Keys, wo er emsig und in aller Abgeschiedenheit an einer großen Serie von Bildern und Zeichnungen arbeitete.

JB: In which way was Emmett Williams connected to Copley, Anthony?

AA: In the late 1960s Williams received a visual arts grant from Copley's philanthropic foundation, the Cassandra Foundation (originally called the William and Noma Copley Foundation). Whatever personal friendship was established was likely made through Dieter Roth, who also facilitated Iannone's contribution (*LBJ*, 1968) to an unrealised seventh issue of Copley's artists' magazine *S.M.S.* In the show you mentioned, in 1993, Williams, Copley and Dorothy Iannone were shown together in *Berliner Amerikaner*, with Copley, I suppose, playing the role as invited guest, since he was not an American

JB: Abgesehen davon, dass Copley und Iannone durch das
starre Raster von Kunstbewegungen fielen, traf ihre Arbeit
auch auf harten Widerstand. Dorothy Iannone hatte häufig
mit Zensur zu kämpfen. Copley rechnete oft damit, blieb aber
letztlich fast immer verschont, sogar als er seine *X-Rated*-Serie
ausstellte. Nur eine einzige Arbeit, die zwei Spritzen zeigt
(*Untitled*, 1962, Menil Collection), musste er abhängen. Wel-
chen Grund hat eurer Meinung nach diese unterschiedliche
Beziehungen zur Öffentlichkeit?

AA: Copley hatte Freude daran, Menschen mit seiner
Arbeit zu schockieren, hauptsächlich aber jene, die Kunst
seiner Meinung nach zu ernst nahmen. Kasper König
sagte kürzlich: „Copley fand, dass man aus Kunst keine
allzu große Sache machen sollte. In seinen Augen sollte
Kunst – trotz ihres hohen Status – nicht so sehr beweih-
räuchert werden."[17] Was die Zensur betrifft, so war die
Bildsprache in seinem Werk zwar oftmals eindeutig
sexuell, etwa in der Reihe *X-Rated*, allerdings nur selten
pornografisch im engeren Sinne. Den Figuren fehlte der
Realismus einer Betty Tompkins' mit ihren *Fuck*-Bildern,
die etwa zur gleichen Zeit wie Copleys *X-Rated*-Serie
entstanden und (in Paris) der gleichen Zensur anheim-
fielen wie Dorothy Iannones Werk. Die unterschiedli-
chen Reaktionen könnten natürlich auch im Geschlecht
begründet liegen. Die Radikalität von Iannones Werk
speist sich zum Teil daraus, dass sie sexuelle Identität
und weibliche Lust zum Thema macht. Das scheint die
meist männlichen Kuratoren und Museumsdirektoren
(und sogar befreundete Künstler) nervös gemacht zu
haben.

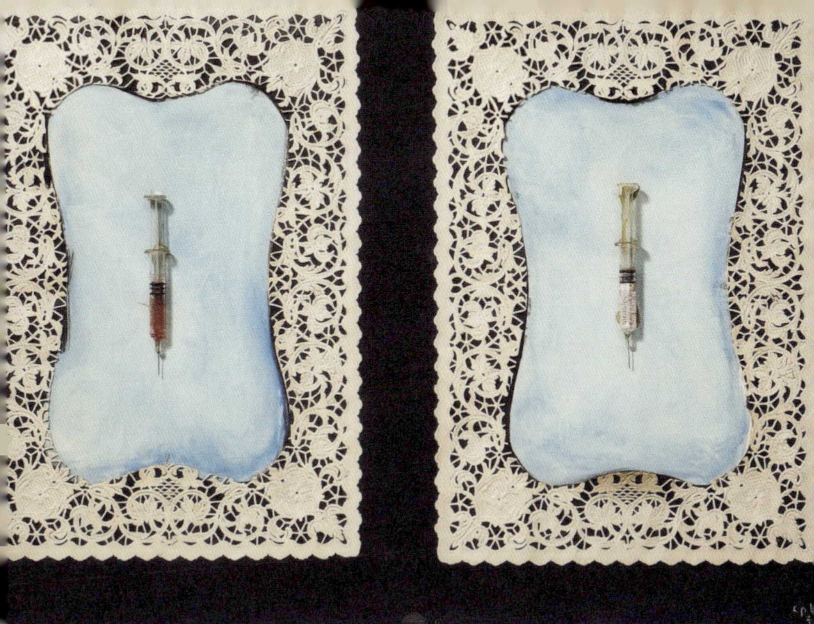

JB: Besides falling through the gaps in the rigid structures of art movements, there was also quite a lot of resistance towards their work. Dorothy Iannone experienced more of the censorship, which in Copley's case, he often anticipated, although it almost never occurred, not even when he exhibited the *X-Rated* series. There was only one case, where two syringes were depicted in his work, that it was taken down (*Untitled*, 1962, Menil Collection). What do you think is the reason for the different relations with the public?

AA: Copley delighted in shocking people with his work, but this tendency was mostly aimed at people who he felt took art too seriously. As Kasper König recently said, '…[Copley] perceived art not with a capital A. For him, art – despite its high status –should not be canonized so much.'[18] Regarding censorship, even when the sexual imagery was most explicit in his work, as in the *X-Rated* series, it was rarely pornographic in any strict sense. The figures lacked the realism of, say, Betty Tompkins' *Fuck* paintings, which were created around the same time as Copley's *X-Rated* series and were subject to the same kind of censorship (in Paris) as Dorothy Iannone's work. The different response could be due to gender too, of course. Part of the radicality of Iannone's work seems to be its assertion of sexual identity and female pleasure, aspects which seemed to have made the mostly male curators and museum directors (and even artist friends) nervous.

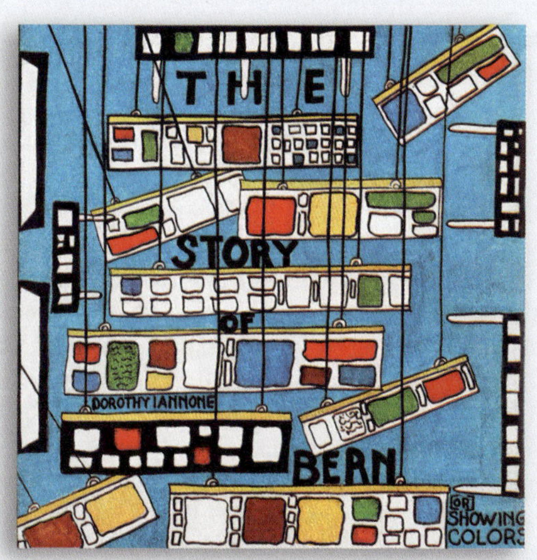

THE
T H E
STORY
OF
DOROTHY IANNONE
BERN
[OR]
SHOWING
COLORS

JB: Apropos Zensur: In der Geschichte *Dorothy Iannone: The Story of Bern, or Showing Colors* (1970), herausgegeben von der Künstlerin selbst, beschreibt sie einen Vorfall im Zusammenhang mit der Ausstellung *Freunde – Friends – d'Fründe* in Bern. Der bekannte Kurator Harald Szeemann lud Karl Gerstner, Dieter Roth, Daniel Spoerri und André Thomkins dazu ein, Werke befreundeter Künstler*innen auszustellen, darunter Iannone. Die Zensur ihres Werks und Roths Protestaktion führten schließlich zu Harald Szeemanns Rücktritt als Direktor der Institution, weil er selbst sich in seiner Arbeit als Kurator zensiert fühlte. Schließlich lief die Ausstellung in Düsseldorf ohne Zensur weiter.

FB: Ja, das war nicht Harald Szeemanns Sternstunde, damals 1969. Er wurde zum Rücktritt gezwungen, nahm aber nie öffentlich Stellung gegen die Zensur von Dorothys Werken, im Gegenteil, er wiegelte zur Selbstzensur auf und versuchte, die Solidarität zwischen den eingeladenen Künstler*innen zu untergraben. Er versuchte Dorothy davon zu überzeugen, die betreffenden Zeichnungen abzudecken, und rüttelte am Band der Freundschaft derjenigen, die er für seine letzte Ausstellung in der Kunsthalle Bern zusammengebracht hatte. Dorothy hat die Geschichte dieser Zensur in einem Satz von 69 Tuschezeichnungen festgehalten, die heute im Hammer Museum in Los Angeles aufbewahrt werden. Dank der Neuauflage des Künstlerinnenbuches von JRP|Editions aus dem Jahr 2020 sind die Tafeln heute gut zugänglich. Das Buch ist ein humorvolles Kunstwerk und ein kraftvolles Zeugnis über den *Male Gaze*.

JB: Speaking of censorship, there is a surprising story, *Dorothy Iannone: The Story of Bern, or Showing Colors* (1970), published by the artist herself, in which she describes an incident connected to the *Freunde – Friends – d'Fründe* exhibition in Bern. The well-known curator Harald Szeemann invited Karl Gerstner, Dieter Roth, Daniel Spoerri and André Thomkins to exhibit artist friends, among them Iannone. The censorship of Iannone's work, and Roth's protest, eventually led to Harald Szeemann's resignation as the director of the institution because he himself felt censored in his work as a curator The exhibition actually then went on uncensored to Düsseldorf.

FB: Yes, Harald Szeemann didn't have the best role in this episode in 1969. He was forced to resign, but he never took a public stand against the censorship of Dorothy's works; on the contrary, he fomented self-censorship and helped to dissolve the solidarity between the invited artists. He tried to convince Dorothy that she should cover up the incriminated drawings, and weakened the chain of friends he had initiated for what was to be his final exhibition at the Kunsthalle Bern. Dorothy recounted the story of this censorship in a set of 69 ink drawings (preserved at the Hammer Museum in Los Angeles), original plates for an artist's book that can be easily found, thanks to JRP|Editions' reissue in 2020. It is a humorous artwork and a forceful testimony on the male gaze.

JB: Stimmt es, Anthony, dass Copley auch nicht gerade viel Unterstützung von Szeemann erhielt?

AA: Er unterstützte ihn. Aber bei seiner Teilnahme an der *documenta 5*, die Szeeman kuratierte, machte Copley unglücklicherweise schlechte Erfahrungen. Acht seiner zehn Flaggen (*„Imaginary Flags for Ten Countries"*, 1972/1972–1991), die Copley dort ausstellte, wurden von den Fahnenmasten vor der Neuen Galerie gestohlen. Auf die Organisator*innen der *documenta* konnte er bei dem Versuch, eine Entschädigung für die verlorenen Kunstwerke zu erhalten, nicht zählen. Die Versicherungsgesellschaft erklärte, die Flaggen seien nicht versichert gewesen, da sie *außerhalb* des Veranstaltungsortes präsentiert worden waren. Ich nehme an, diese Odyssee hinterließ bei Copley einen bitteren Nachgeschmack. In bestimmten Fragen des Kunstgeschäfts konnte er eine ziemliche Professionalität an den Tag legen und erwartete von Szeemans Team wahrscheinlich eine bessere Behandlung.

JB: Anthony, is it true, that Copley might also not have earned much support from Szeemann?

AA: He was supportive, but Copley had bad luck with his experience participating in *documenta 5*, which Szeemann curated. Eight of the ten editioned flags (*Imaginary Flags for Ten Countries*, 1972/1972–1991) loaned to the exhibition by Copley were stolen off their flagpoles in front of the Neue Galerie building. The *documenta* organisers were unhelpful in reimbursing the costs of Copley's lost artworks. The insurance company declared since they were exhibited *outside* of the venue, they were not subject to coverage. I assume this whole ordeal left a bad taste for Copley, who could be quite professional in certain art business matters and probably expected better treatment from Szeemann's team.

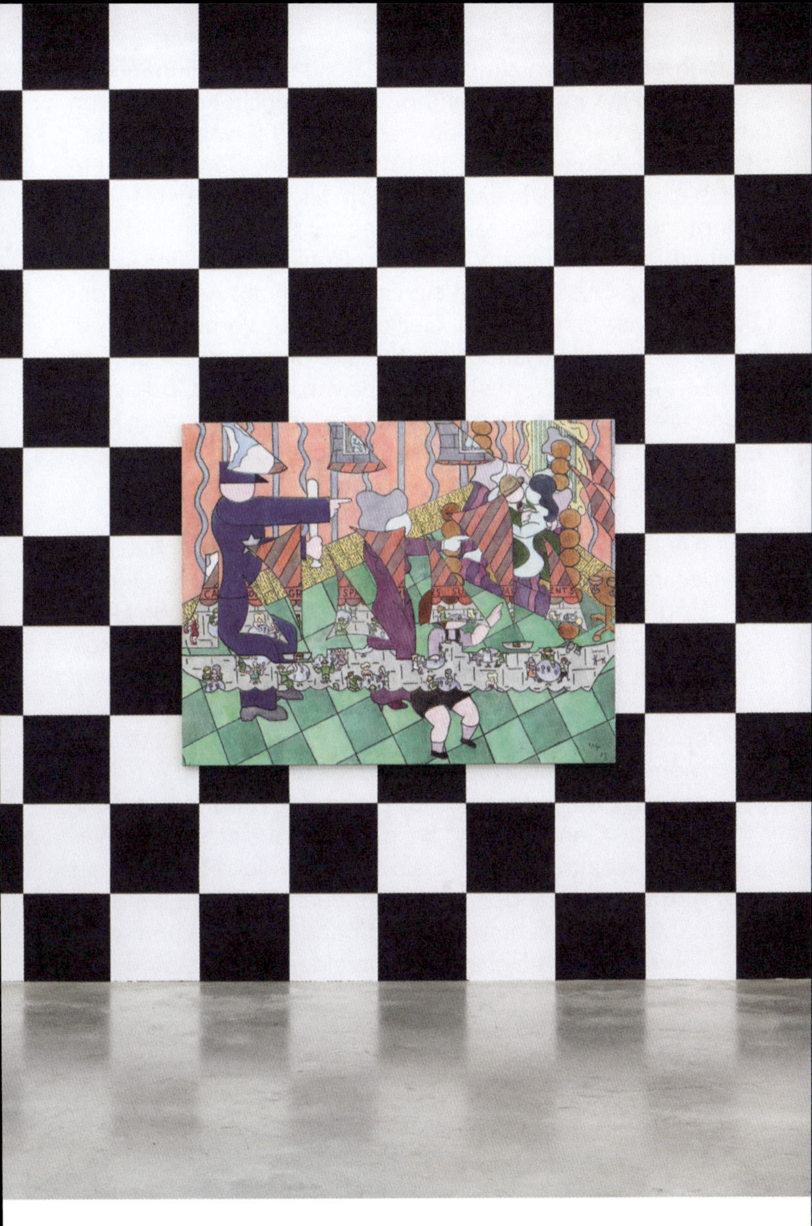

JB: In ihrem offenen Umgang mit Sexualität bedienen sich Copley und Iannone ganz unterschiedlicher Stereotypen von Geschlecht, die, wie ich finde, beide hoch relevante Aspekte der heutigen Geschlechterpolitik aufgreifen: Copley arbeitet mit Übertreibungen. In seinen Bildern sind die Geschlechterstereotypen oft so überzeichnet, dass wir uns ihnen und ihrer Ernsthaftigkeit ab einem gewissen Punkt nicht mehr sicher sein können. Er beschäftigt sich aber auch mit Aspekten der (Selbst)Bestrafung (Polizei, Guillotine) und -Vernichtung – in *The Story of my Life* landet der Künstler sogar selbst unterm Fallbeil. Anthony, du hast einmal erwähnt, dass Copley mit Tropen und klischeehaften Charakteren arbeitet, in einem Maß, dass man hier regelrecht von einer Loslösung von Geschlecht sprechen könnte. Was meinst du damit?

AA: Copley inszenierte seine Charaktere als Schauspieler*innen in seiner eigenen *Commedia dell'arte*. Diesen Begriff borgte er sich, um eine improvisatorische Situation zu beschreiben, in der die Verwendung wiederkehrender Bilder als „Sprungbrett" für das Schaffen neuer Bedeutungen dienen kann.[19] Auf persönlicher Ebene spiegelte Copleys Arbeit oft eine Reaktion auf das repressive Umfeld seiner Kindheit und Jugend wider. Er scherzte einmal, seine Ausstellung *X-Rated* (New York Cultural Center, 1974) sei möglicherweise ein Versuch der „Selbsttherapie".[20] Viele Arbeiten, die im Laufe seiner Karriere entstanden, enthalten auch Fetisch-Elemente: echte Damenschuhe, Strumpfbandschnallen und natürlich collagierte Spitze, ein charakteristisches Motiv seines Werks. Doch Copleys weibliche Figuren sind selten Objekte seiner Begierde. Die Obsessivität und Regelmäßigkeit, mit der er diese figurale Bildsprache einsetzt, spricht eher für einen, wie Celant es nannte, „selbst-referenziellen" und expressiven Modus in Copleys Werk.[21] Männliche und weibliche Figuren kämpfen, umarmen sich, verschmelzen, tauschen Körperteile aus. Copley

überspitzte Geschlecht satirisch, ja, aber er füllte seine Bilder auch mit Signifikanten des Femininen, was auf
eine erotische oder psychologische Identifikation mit
dem anderen Geschlecht hindeutet.

JB: In their openness about sexuality, one may find a very different use of gender stereotypes – both of which, I would argue,
are extremely relevant aspects in today's gender politics: In
Copley's images, you may find aspects of exaggeration of gender stereotypes to a point where one cannot be sure of it, of
its seriousness, but he also engages with aspects of (self-)
punishment (the police, the guillotine) and cancellation (in
The Story of my Life the artist himself actually gets guillotined).
Anthony – you mentioned that Copley engages in tropes and
stock characters, so much so that this might even be a detach-
ment from gender – what do you mean by this?

> AA: Copley conceived of his stock characters as play-
> ers in his own *commedia dell'arte*, borrowing the term
> to describe an improvisatory situation where the use of
> recurring images can serve as a 'jumping-off place' for
> creating new meanings.[22] On a personal level, Copley's
> work often reflected a response to the repressive envi-
> ronment of his childhood and adolescence. He quipped
> that his *X-Rated* exhibition (New York Cultural Center,
> 1974) might be an attempt at 'self-therapy'.[23] Many works
> made throughout his career also incorporate fetish ele-
> ments: real women's shoes, garter-belt buckles, and of
> course, collaged lace, a signature motif in his work. But
> Copley's female figures are rarely objects of his desire
> – the obsessiveness and repetitiveness with which
> Copley incorporates this figural imagery points to what
> Celant described as a 'self-referential' and expressive
> mode in Copley's work.[24] Male and female figures bat-
> tle, embrace, merge, swap parts. Copley satirised gen-
> der, yes, but he also immersed his imagery in feminine

JB: In Dorothy Iannones Arbeit liegt der Fokus viel eher auf der „ekstatischen Einheit", wie sie gegenüber Maurizio Cattelan einmal in einem Interview sagte, auf dem Zelebrieren von Geschlecht und insbesondere der weiblichen Lust. Nach ihrer Teilnahme an der 4. Berliner Biennale 2006 wurde Iannones Werk von einer jüngeren Generation von Kurator*innen wiederentdeckt, die diese Aspekte ihres Schaffens und deren Bedeutsamkeit für das Publikum herausstellten. Schauen wir uns einmal das wunderbare Bild *I Have Got Such a Marvelous Cock* aus unserer Ausstellung an, ein Werk aus ihrer *Eros*-Reihe (1969/70). Der Schwerpunkt der gezeigten Werke, sowohl Copleys als Iannones, liegt zwar hauptsächlich auf *weißer* Heteronormativität, aber sie haben auch eine Offenheit an sich, die weiter reicht. Im erwähnten Beispiel findet durch die Überlappung der Genitalien des Paares eine Art Verschmelzung der Geschlechter statt, etwas jenseits des Binären. Und Iannones gemalte und gezeichnete äußere Vulvalippen erinnern in ihren Maßen fast an Hoden. Florence, in welchem Umfeld wuchs Iannone auf?

FB: Dorothy wuchs in einem heteronormativen, *weißen* Arbeitermilieu auf und besuchte dann die Universität – ebenfalls ein überwiegend heteronormatives und *weißes* Umfeld. Aber sie war sehr freisinnig, hatte keine Angst vor Sex und war offen für Erfahrungen aller Art. Obwohl sie ihre Sinnlichkeit frei zur Schau stellte und nie verbarg, war sie im Grunde eine Mystikerin (eine marxistische Mystikerin sogar), und es ist nicht überraschend, dass sie sich in den 1980er Jahren dem Tantrismus zuwandte (wie auch Filliou). In Iannones Werk kommen freudvolle Sinnlichkeit, die Verherrlichung fleischlicher Freuden und ein gesundes Maß provokativen Spaßes zusammen. Es ist kaum in Worte zu fassen, wie eifrig sie innerhalb fest abgesteckter

Grenzen herumtobte und Possen trieb, wobei sie sogar in dem „künstlerischen" Umfeld, das sich in der WASP-Gesellschaft bildete, noch aneckte.[25] Ihre Werke wurden wiederholt zensiert, sie kämpfte gegen diese Zensur an, erwirkte die Einfuhr von Henry Millers Büchern in die USA – und mit Sicherheit genoss sie ihre Rolle als Kriegerin in einem permanenten Kampf gegen Selbstgerechtigkeit.

JB: In Dorothy Iannone's work, on the other hand, there is a much greater focus on 'ecstatic unity', as she once told Maurizio Cattelan in an interview, on celebratory aspects of gender and especially on female pleasure. Following her participation in the 4th Berlin Biennale in 2006, Iannone's work was rediscovered late by a younger generation of curators, who highlighted these aspects of her works and their importance to the audience. Let's look, for example, at the wonderful painting from our show, *I Have Got Such a Marvelous Cock* (from the *Eros Paintings* series) (1969/70). While the works in the exhibition, by both Copley and Iannone, are mostly focused on white heteronormativity, there is also an openness to them that reaches further. In the example mentioned, you might find a merging of gender, something beyond the binary, in the overlapping of this couples' genitals. And Iannone's painted and drawn outer labia might even seem reminiscent of testicles. Florence, what environment did Iannone grow up in?

FB: Dorothy grew up in a heteronormative, white, working-class environment, then went to university, predominantly heteronormative and white there too. But she was very liberated, with no fear of sex, and was open to all experiences. While her sensuality was unmistakable and never hidden, she was fundamentally a mystic (even a Marxist mystic), and it's not surprising that she turned to Tantrism in the 1980s (as did Filliou).

In Iannone's work, joyful sensuality, glorification of carnal pleasures and a healthy dose of provocative fun all come together. There's no telling how much she romped and frolicked in a constrained universe, even in the 'artistic' milieu that evolved in WASP society.[26] She was repeatedly censored, fought against censorship, helped get Henry Miller's books distributed in the USA – and she certainly also took pleasure in the role of warrior in a permanent struggle against self-righteousness.

JB: Sowohl Iannone als auch Copley veröffentlichten mehrere Bücher. Neben ihrem Einsatz für die Arbeit von Henry Miller gab Iannone selbst eine bemerkenswerte Menge detaillierter Einblicke in ihr Privatleben, sogar in die intimsten Momente: 1968 veröffentlichte sie ein Künstlerinnenbuch mit dem Titel *Lists (IV): A More Detailed Than Requested Reconstruction – from The Book of D & D* (1968), das eine Liste aller Männer enthielt, mit denen sie geschlafen hatte – eine Zusammenstellung, die entstand, nachdem Diether Roth sich nach ihren früheren sexuellen Beziehungen erkundigt hatte. Allgemein sind ihre Arbeiten voller Geschichten über Liebende und Romanzen, die einen Bezug zu ihrem Privatleben haben. Auch William Copley gab viele Schriften über sein Privatleben heraus und schuf Werke, die seinen sechs Ehefrauen gewidmet waren. Wie reagierte Copleys Umfeld darauf?

AA: Interessanterweise wurde Copleys Arbeit zu Lebzeiten gut aufgenommen und seine Ausstellungen erhielten fast immer positive Kritiken in der *New York Times, im Artforum* und anderswo. Die Kunstwelt – zumindest die Kunstjournalist*innen – reagierte mit enorm viel Zuspruch. In seiner Familie war Copley das schwarze Schaf. Seine Auswanderung nach Frankreich in den 1950er Jahren kann in gewisser Weise als Bruch mit seinem familiären Umfeld verstanden werden (obwohl er durch Erbschaft Anteilseigner der Copley Press blieb und mehrere Jahre lang weiterhin für die Zeitungen der Familie arbeitete). Copleys Familie, insbesondere sein Bruder James,

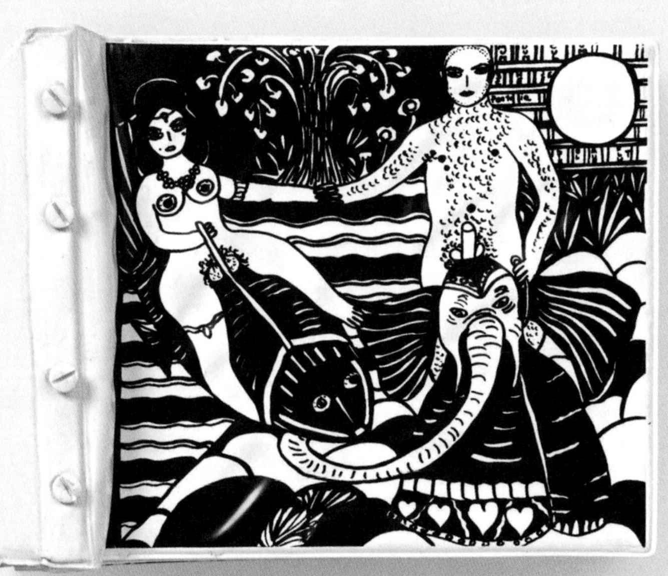

blickte möglicherweise mit einem gewissen Grad an Ver-
dutztheit auf seine künstlerischen Aktivitäten.

JB: Yes, both Iannone and Copley published several books.
Besides Iannone advocating the work of Henry Miller, she also
published an unusual amount of detailed insights into her private life, even the most intimate moments: In 1968 Iannone
published an artist's book called *Lists (IV): A More Detailed
Than Requested Reconstruction – from The Book of D & D*
(1968), which contained a list of all the men she had slept with,
compiled after Diether Roth inquired about her previous sexual relations; and in her works you may find many stories of
lovers, and romances connected to her personal life. William
Copley also published many writings on his private life and
made works dedicated to his six wives. How did Copley's sur-
rounding environment respond to this?

> AA: Well, interestingly, Copley's work was critically well
> received during his lifetime, and his exhibitions almost
> always received positive reviews in the *New York Times*,
> *Artforum*, and other venues. The response of the art world
> was – at least from art journalists – highly supportive.
> Among his family, Copley was the black sheep. His expa-
> triation to France in the 1950s could be seen as a cut-
> ting-of-ties in a way (though he remained a shareholder,
> by inheritance, in the Copley Press, as well as a contrib-
> utor to the family's newspapers for several more years).
> Copley's family – namely his brother James – probably
> viewed his artistic pursuits with a degree of bafflement.

JB: In seiner Kindheit ging Copley auf eine katholische Schule,
und Iannone bezeichnete sich wiederholt als Sünderin und
berichtete davon, wie sie jeden Samstag vor dem sonntägli-
chen Gottesdienst zur Beichte gehen zu musste. Welche Rolle
spielen die katholische Kirche und die organisierte Religion
im Allgemeinen im Œuvre der beiden?

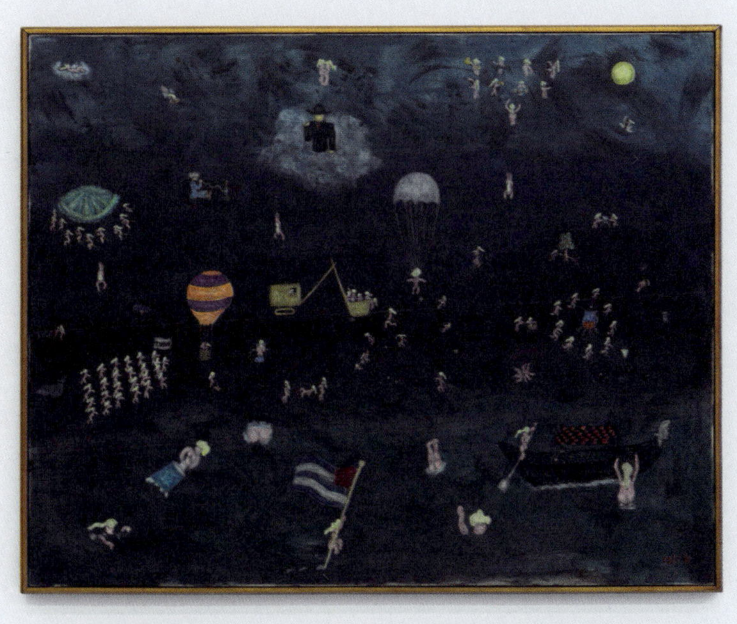

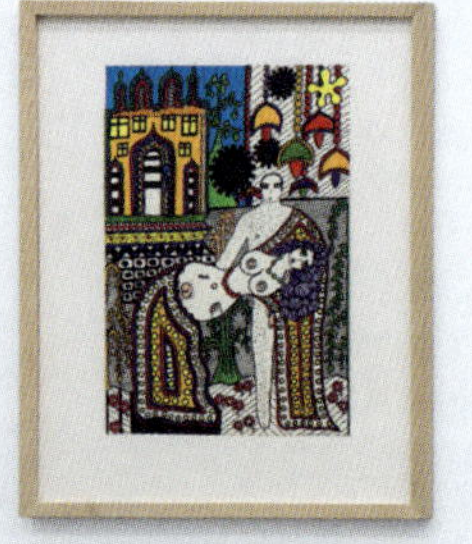 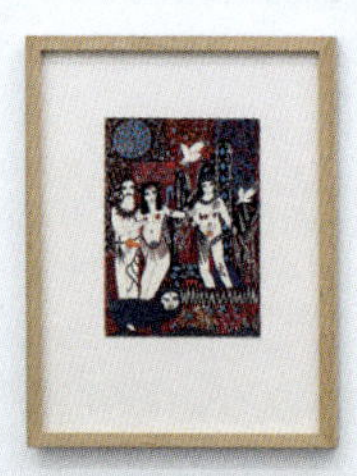

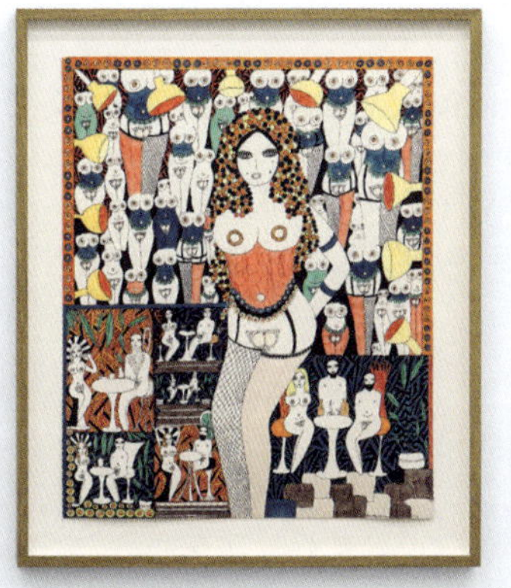 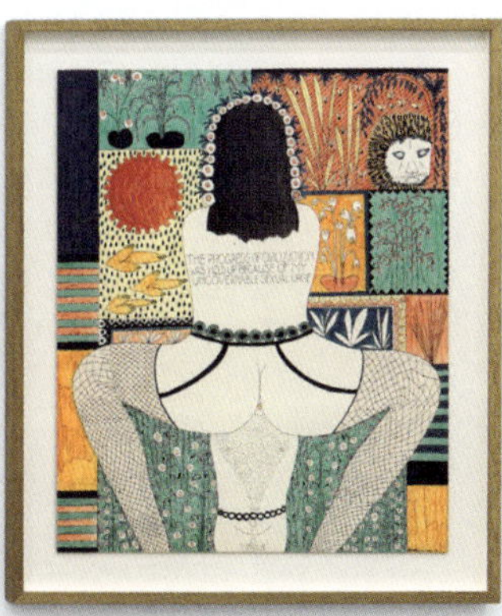

AA: Verweise auf die Kirche sind in Copleys Werk all-gegenwärtig. Seine Phrase *trust lust/heed greed* („wol-le Lust/hab Gier"), die in mehreren seiner Bilder und Titel erscheint, ist sein eigenes, Grenzen überschreiten-des Anti-Gebot. Generell lieferten die Erzählungen des Neuen und Alten Testaments Copley endloses Quellen-material. Er liebte es, respektlose Bilder von Adam und Eva zu malen, in denen er den Verlust der Unschuld im Garten Eden und Vorstellungen vom Paradies zitierte.

FB: Religiöse Zwänge machen das Übertreten von Gren-zen reizvoller und vergnüglicher! Das Cloisonné in Dorothys Bildern hat etwas von den Buntglasfenstern katholischer Kirchen. Ich empfehle das Interview mit Noa Jones zu diesem Thema, in dem Dorothy frei über ihre Beziehung zur katholischen Religion, Spiritualität, den gnostischen Evangelien und Dharma spricht.[27]

JB: Moreover, with Copley having been to a Catholic school, and Iannone repeatedly referring to herself as a sinner and mentioning having to go to confession every Saturday before church service on Sunday, what part do the Catholic Church and organised religion in general play in their respective œuvre?

AA: Signifiers of the Church are ubiquitous in Copley's oeuvre and Copley's phrase *Trust lust / heed greed*, which appeared in several of his paintings and titles, is his own transgressive anti-commandment. More gener-ally, the narratives of the New and Old Testaments pro-vided Copley with endless source material. He loved to paint irreverent images of Adam and Eve, invoking the loss of innocence in the Garden of Eden, and ideas of Paradise.

JB: Interessant ist auch, dass Iannone, die Berlin liebte und dort bis zu ihrem Tod 2022 lebte, in der Stadt positiv (wenn auch eher spät) wahrgenommen wurde, während in den 1960er Jahren noch große Skepsis gegenüber ihrer Arbeit herrschte. Copley hingegen ist in Deutschland ein renommierter Künstler. Obwohl er nicht hier lebte, pflegte er eine enge Beziehung zu Walther König, und seine Werke werden in Deutschland und Umgebung rege gesammelt. Was glaubt ihr, inwiefern haben die beiden beim deutschen Publikum einen Nerv getroffen?

AA: Nachdem ich erst kürzlich Zeit in Deutschland verbracht und mit Sammler*innen über seine Arbeit gesprochen habe, habe ich mir dieses Thema noch einmal durch den Kopf gehen lassen. Ich denke, die Erklärung ist im Grunde ganz simpel. Die deutsche Kultur ist bekannt für die Werte Disziplin, Ordnung und Respekt. Copleys Arbeiten zelebrieren genau das Gegenteil: Freiheit, Vergnügen und provokativen Humor. Befürworter*innen von Copleys Werk in Deutschland, wenn ich hier verallgemeinern darf, lieben diese Dimension seiner Arbeit. Sie kennen sich aus mit den Fesseln des Konservatismus und der Orthodoxie, die Copleys Arbeit von ganzem Herzen ablehnt. Auch ist das deutsche Publikum kunstgeschichtlich bewandert und wertschätzt Copleys einzigartige Rolle als Unruhestifter und Vordenker.

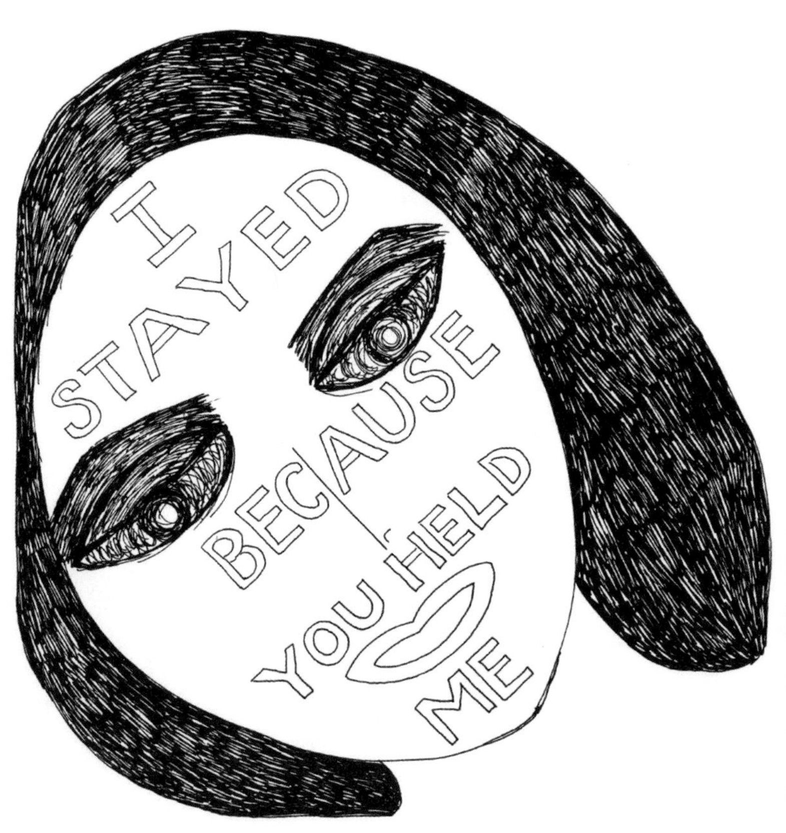
I STAYED
BECAUSE
YOU HELD ME

BECAUSE I WANTED TO REFORM GERMANY

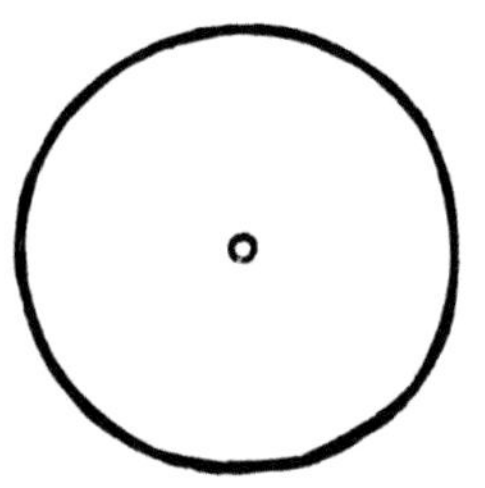

And I cannot say that another country will evoke a different song.

FB: Dorothy selbst lachte manchmal darüber, und in ihrer Serie *An Explosive Interlude* (1979) stellt sie genau diese Frage, die in den letzten beiden der 13 Zeichnungen beantwortet wird. Dort heißt es:

„Well I stayed
I stayed because you held me
Because I wanted to reform Germany
And I cannot say that another country will evoke a different song."[29]

JB: It is also interesting to mention that Iannone, who loved Berlin and lived there until her passing in 2022, has been received well (but rather late) in Berlin, while there was a lot of scepticism towards her work in the 1960s. Copley, however, is a very renowned artist in Germany. Despite not having lived here, he was closely connected to Walther König, and since then has been collected intensively in and around Germany. In what ways, would you think, did they hit a nerve for their German audience?

AA: Having just spent time in Germany talking to collectors about his work, I have given this some new thought and think it comes down to a rather basic theory. German culture is known for its values of discipline, order, and respectfulness. Copley's work celebrates the opposite tendency, promoting freedom, pleasure, and provocative humour. Advocates of Copley's work in Germany, if I may generalise here, love this dimension in the work. They know better than anyone the limits of conservatism and orthodoxy, which Copley's work wholeheartedly rejects. German audiences are also finely attuned to art history and can recognise Copley's singular role as an agitator and original.

FB: She herself sometimes laughed about it, and the set of drawings *An Explosive Interlude* (1979) asks exactly that question, which is answered in the last two in the series of thirteen drawings. They state:

'Well I stayed
I stayed because you held me
Because I wanted to reform Germany
And I cannot say that another country will evoke a different song.'

JB: Oh, wie wunderbar! Ich bin mir sicher, dass ihre und Copleys Arbeiten auch weiterhin ausgestellt und Eindruck hinterlassen werden. Abschließend möchte ich darauf zu sprechen kommen, dass ihr beiden die Estates dieser großartigen Künstler*innen leitet. Auf welche Weise steht ihr mit den Familien der beiden in Verbindung?

AA: Ich arbeite eng mit der Familie Copley zusammen, die sich mit der Arbeit ihres Vaters bestens auskennt. Ich danke ihnen dafür, dass sie meine Forschung in den letzten zehn Jahren, seit ich gemeinsam mit ihnen die Arbeit an diesem laufenden Projekt aufgenommen habe, unterstützt und mir ihr Vertrauen geschenkt haben. Billy Copley, der Sohn, ist selbst ein sachkundiger Künstler, Claire Copley betrieb in den 1970er Jahren eine bedeutende Galerie für Konzeptkunst in Los Angeles und die jüngere Schwester der beiden, Theodora, befasst sich mit viel Leidenschaft und Scharfsinn mit der Arbeit ihres Vaters. Sie verstehen es hervorragend, sich um sein Erbe zu kümmern.

FB: Dorothy hat keine Blutsverwandten, sondern eine Familie im Herzen, bestehend aus Künstler*innen auf der einen und begeisterten Praktizierenden des tibetischen Buddhismus auf der anderen Seite. Ich bin natürlich

Mitglied des künstlerischen Teils der Familie. Als solches arbeite ich mit ihren Freund*innen Jan Voss und Henriette van Egten (Boekie Woekie) zusammen, aber ich habe auch eine Spende für einen Meditationsraum mit wunderschönem Altar im Dharma Mati, einem Rigpa-Zentrum in Berlin, organisiert.

JB: Oh, that's wonderful. I am sure her work and Copley's will continue to be exhibited and have an effect on us! To conclude, you are both running the estates of these two amazing artists. In which ways are you connected to the families of the artists?

AA: I work closely with the Copley family, who are experts in their father's work. I thank them for supporting and trusting my research over the last ten years since I have been working with them on this ongoing project. Billy Copley, the artist's son, is a knowledgeable artist, Claire Copley had operated an important Conceptual Art gallery in Los Angeles the 1970s, and their younger sister, Theodora, is extremely passionate and perceptive about her father's work. They are great people to look after this legacy.

FB: Dorothy doesn't have a blood family, but a heart family, made up of artists on the one hand, and assiduous practitioners of Tibetan Buddhism on the other. I am obviously part of the family of artists. As such, I now work in complicity with her friends Jan Voss and Henriette van Egten (Boekie Woekie), but I also organised the donation of a meditation room, including a beautiful altar, to Dharma Mati, the Rigpa centre in Berlin.

JB: Bitte erzählt uns doch etwas mehr über die aktuelle Arbeit eurer Estates und deren Ziele für die absehbare Zukunft!

FB: Dorothy wählte mich persönlich aus, die Arbeit fortzusetzen, die ich als Leiterin der Galerie Air de Paris, die sie seit 2006 vertritt, begonnen hatte. Ich werde mich jetzt den Archiven widmen, sie teils aufarbeiten und teils bei passenden öffentlichen Sammlungen unterbringen. Es ist wichtig, dass alle problemlos darauf zugreifen können. Ein bedeutender Teil des Archivs wird der Berlinischen Galerie übergeben; er zeugt von der Kunstwelt in Düsseldorf und Berlin der letzten 50 Jahre. Ich arbeite derzeit mit Joanna Zielinska an der Monografie zur Ausstellung *Love Is Forever Isn't It*? am M HKA Museum für Zeitgenössische Kunst Antwerpen. Auch in den USA möchte ich Türen öffnen. Außerdem veröffentliche ich die Arbeit von Dorothys Mutter, Sarah Pucci.

AA: Wir holen laufend Informationen von ehemaligen oder aktuellen Eigentümer*innen bisher nicht gefundener Copley-Werke für unsere Forschungsdatenbank ein. Das ist eine Art interner Catalogue raisonné für Kurator*innen, Händler*innen und Forschende, die an seiner Arbeit interessiert sind. Ein großes, für die nahe Zukunft geplantes Projekt ist eine umfassende monografische Studie über die Copley Galleries von Mark Nelson (Autor von *Hollywood Arensberg*, 2020), der derzeit Korrespondenzen und Unterlagen für eine nahezu originalgetreue Neugestaltung aller sechs von der Galerie gezeigten Ausstellungen zusammenträgt. Die Detailtiefe ist atemberaubend und wird eine Fülle erhellender Informationen über diese mittlerweile legendäre Galerie in LA County ans Licht bringen. Vor kurzem, im Frühjahr 2024, präsentierten wir *William N. Copley: LXCN CPLY* in der Kasmin in New York – eine Einzelausstellung, die sich mit seinem persönlichen Lexikon aus charakteristischen Motiven und Bildern befasst.

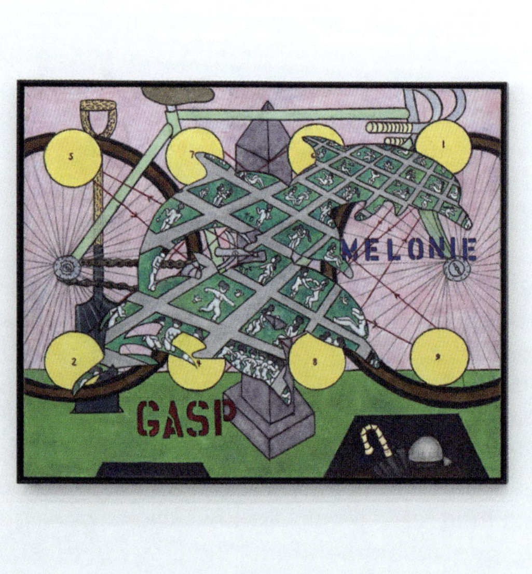

MELONIE
GASP

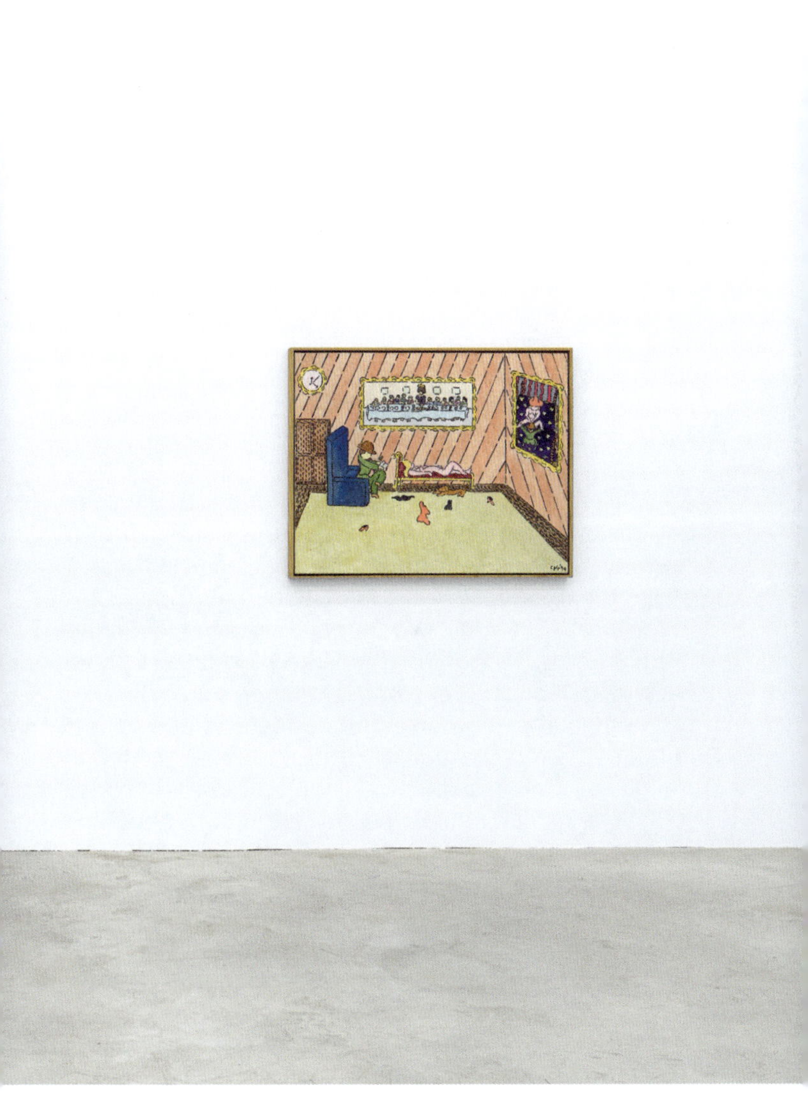

JB: Oh, please tell us more about the current work of the estate and what its goals for the foreseeable future are!

FB: Dorothy personally chose me to continue the work begun as director of the Air de Paris gallery, which has represented her since 2006. I'm now going to work on the archives, treating some of them and placing others in appropriate public collections. It is important that everyone gets easy access to them. An important part of this archive is being donated to the Berlinische Galerie; it bears witness to the art world in Düsseldorf and Berlin over the last 50 years. I am currently working with Joanna Zielinska on the monograph accompanying the exhibition *Love Is Forever Isn't It*? at the M HKA (Museum of Contemporary Art) in Antwerp. I wish to open more doors in the USA. I'm also distributing the work of her mother, Sarah Pucci.

AA: We are continuously soliciting information from past or current owners of unlocated Copley works for our research database, which serves as a kind of internal raisonné for curators, dealers, and researchers interested in the work. One major forthcoming project is a definitive monographic study on the Copley Galleries by Mark Nelson (author of *Hollywood Arensberg*, 2020) who is currently compiling correspondence and documentation for a near recreation of all six shows presented by the gallery. The level of detail is mind-blowing and will bring to light a trove of revelatory information about this now legendary LA gallery. Recently, in spring 2024, we presented *William N. Copley: LXCN CPLY* at Kasmin in New York – a one-person exhibition focusing on the artist's personal lexicon of signature motifs and images.

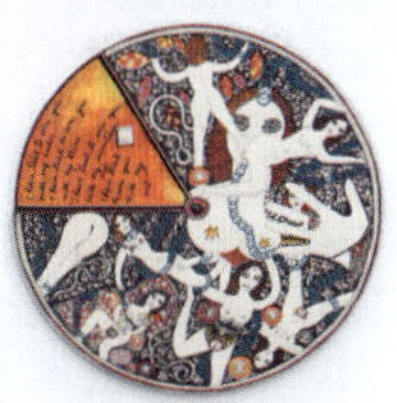

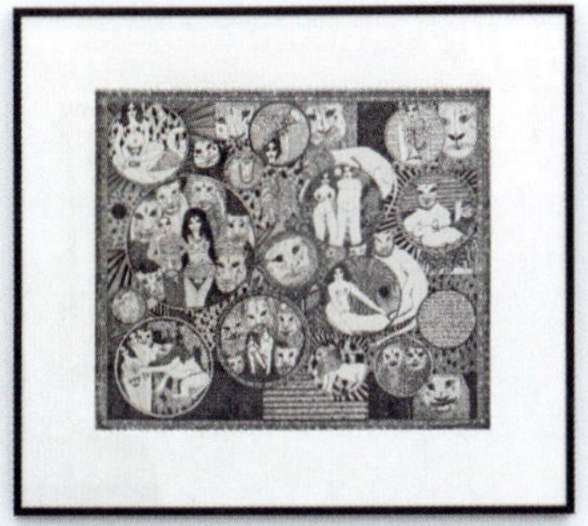

JB: Vielen Dank! Es war großartig, Einblicke aus den Estates zu erhalten. Wir schätzen eure Expertise und euren Einsatz für die Arbeit der beiden Künstler*innen sehr.

FB: Vielen Dank auch für den schönen Titel eurer Ausstellung! Er erinnert mich an den Film *Only Lovers Left Alive* (Jim Jarmusch, 2013), den Dorothy so gerne mochte.

JB: Thank you very much, it was wonderful to get insights from both the estates and we really appreciate the understanding and dedication you give to the artists' work!

FB: Thank you also for the beautiful title of your exhibition, which reminds me of *Only Lovers Left Alive* (Jim Jarmusch, 2013), which Dorothy liked so much!

1   Siehe auch: „Cummings Interview",
in *William N. Copley: Selected Writings*,
Hrsg. Anthony Atlas (Köln: Buchhandlung
Walther König, 2020), S. 133
2   „Fremont Interview", in *William N.
Copley: Selected Writings*, Hrsg. Anthony
Atlas (Köln: Buchhandlung Walther König,
2020), S. 168
3   See also: 'Cummings Interview', in
William N. Copley: Selected Writings, ed.
Anthony Atlas (Cologne: Buchhandlung
Walther König, 2020), p. 133.
4   'Fremont Interview', in *William N.
Copley: Selected Writings*, ed. Anthony
Atlas (Cologne: Buchhandlung Walther
König, 2020), p. 168.
5   „Portrait of the Artist as a Young
Dealer", in *William N. Copley: Selected
Writings*, Hrsg. Anthony Atlas (Köln:
Buchhandlung Walther König, 2020), S. 64
6   Tanning, Dorothea, *Dorothea Tanning
to Joseph Cornell, 1947 April 29*, Joseph
Cornell Papers, 1804–1986, Archives of
American Art, Smithsonian Institution
7   „About the Hare and the Tortoise but
Mostly About the Hare", in *William N.
Copley: Selected Writings*, Hrsg. Anthony
Atlas (Köln: Buchhandlung Walther König,
2020), S. 99
8   'Portrait of the Artist as a Young
Dealer', in *William N. Copley: Selected
Writings*, ed. Anthony Atlas (Cologne:
Buchhandlung Walther König, 2020), p. 64.
9   Tanning, Dorothea, *Dorothea Tanning
to Joseph Cornell, 1947 April 29*, Joseph
Cornell papers, 1804-1986. Archives of
American Art, Smithsonian Institution.
10   'About the Hare and the Tortoise
but Mostly About the Hare', in *William N.
Copley: Selected Writings*, ed. Anthony
Atlas (Cologne: Buchhandlung Walther
König, 2020), p. 99
11   Iannone, Dorothy, *A Fluxus Essay*,
(Berlin: Tochnit Aleph, 1979/2016).
12   Celant, Germano et al. (Hrsg.), *William
N. Copley* (Mailand, Houston: Fondazione
Prada and the Menil Collection), S. 15
13   „Fremont interview", in *William N.
Copley: Selected Writings*, Hrsg. Anthony
Atlas (Köln: Buchhandlung Walther König,
2020), S. 165
14   Iannone, Dorothy, *A Fluxus Essay*,
(Berlin: Tochnit Aleph, 1979/2016).

15   Celant, Germano (ed.) et al., *William N. Copley*, (Milano, Houston: Fondazione Prada and the Menil Collection) p. 15.
16   'Fremont interview', in *William N. Copley: Selected Writings*, ed. Anthony Atlas (Cologne: Buchhandlung Walther König, 2020), p. 165.
17   Seidel, Stephanie, König, Kasper „On William N. Copley: Kasper König in Conversation with Stephanie Seidel", in *William N. Copley: The Coffin They Carry You Off In* (Miami: ICA Miami, 2019)
18   Seidel, Stephanie, König, Kasper, 'On William N. Copley: Kasper König in Conversation with Stephanie Seidel', in *William N. Copley: The Coffin They Carry You Off In* (Miami: ICA Miami, 2019).
19   „Alan Jones interview", in *William N. Copley: Selected Writings*, Hrsg. Anthony Atlas (Köln: Buchhandlung Walther König, 2020), S. 189
20   „Sam Hunter interview", in *William N. Copley: Selected Writings*, Hrsg. Anthony Atlas (Köln: Buchhandlung Walther König, 2020), S. 155
21   Celant, Germano (Hrsg.) et al., *William N. Copley* (Mailand, Houston: Fondazione Prada and the Menil Collection), S. 15
22   'Alan Jones interview', in *William N. Copley: Selected Writings*, ed. Anthony Atlas (Cologne: Buchhandlung Walther König, 2020), p. 189.
23   'Sam Hunter interview', in *William N. Copley: Selected Writings*, ed. Anthony Atlas (Cologne: Buchhandlung Walther König, 2020), p. 155.
24   Celant, Germano (ed.) et al., *William N. Copley*, (Milano, Houston: Fondazione Prada and the Menil Collection) p. 15.
25   WASP ist ein Akronym für „White Anglo-Saxon Protestants", ein Begriff für die protestantische weiße Mittel- und Oberschicht der USA.
26   WASP is an acronym for White Anglo-Saxon Protestants.
27   Jones, Noa, „An Interview with Dorothy Iannone. Q&A with a Buddhist artist", in *Tricycle: The Buddhist Review* (Frühjahr 2013): https://tricycle.org/magazine/interview-dorothy-iannone-2/

28   Jones, Noa, 'An Interview with Dorothy Iannone. Q&A with a Buddhist artist', *Tricycle: The Buddhist Review* (Spring 2013): https://tricycle.org/magazine/interview-dorothy-iannone-2/.
29   Deutsche Übersetzung: „Nun, ich blieb Ich blieb, weil ihr mich gehalten habt Weil ich Deutschland reformieren wollte Und ich kann nicht sagen, dass ein anderes Land ein anderes Lied wird erklingen lassen"

27
Dorothy Iannone
*Love Is Forever Isn't It
(The Eternal Calendar)*
1980
© The Estate Of Dorothy Iannone
Leihgabe von Courtesy of Sammlung
Philara, Düsseldorf

28; 29
Dorothy Iannone
Miss My Muse
2000
© The Estate Of Dorothy Iannone, mit
freundlicher Genehmigung der ahlers
collection with friendy permission of
ahlers collection

31
Dorothy Iannone
LBJ
1968, unveröffentlicht unpublished
© The Estate Of Dorothy Iannone
Leihgabe von Courtesy of
William N. Copley Estate

32; 33; 63; 90; 91
Dorothy Iannone
See Yourself as Lovers See You
Installationsansicht Installation View,
Sammlung Philara
© The Estate of Dorothy Iannone

36
William N. Copley
Portrait
October 1970
Photo: Photographer unknown
© William N. Copley Estate

38; 39
William N. Copley
The Evil I ... or the Story of My Life
1965
© William N. Copley Estate
VG Bild-Kunst, Bonn
Leihgabe von Courtesy of Linn Lühn,
Düsseldorf

42
William N. Copley
See Yourself as Lovers See You
1987
© William N. Copley Estate
VG Bild-Kunst, Bonn
Leihgabe von Courtesy of
Galerie Friese, Berlin
Photo: Eric Tschernow, Berlin

45; 100
William N. Copley
Dance of the Hours
1990
© William N. Copley Estate
VG Bild-Kunst, Bonn
Leihgabe von Courtesy of Stiftung der
bewohnte Garten, Pulheim

45; 47
William N. Copley
Acrobats
© William N. Copley Estate
VG Bild-Kunst, Bonn
Leihgabe von Courtesy of Galerie
Friese, Berlin

46
William N. Copley
Nous Deux
ca. 1958-1960
© William N. Copley Estate
VG Bild-Kunst, Bonn
Leihgabe von Courtesy of Galerie
Friese, Berlin
© Photo: 2022 Christie's Images Limited

48
William N. Copley
Towering Inferno
Dokument der ersten Version des
Gemäldes vor der „Selbstzensur" durch
den Künstler, first state of painting
documented prior to Copley's 'self-
censorship' of the work, 1975
© William N. Copley Estate
VG Bild-Kunst, Bonn

101
William N. Copley
Ohne Titel
1994
© William N. Copley Estate
VG Bild-Kunst, Bonn
Leihgabe von Courtesy of Galerie
Friese, Berlin

103
Dorothy Iannone
*Lions For Dieter Rot The Present Lion
Master*
1971
© The Estate Of Dorothy Iannone
Leihgabe von Courtesy of Barbara Wien

103
Dorothy Iannone
I Have Tried to Win You
1978
© The Estate Of Dorothy Iannone, mit
freundlicher Genehmigung der ahlers
collection with friendy permission of the
ahlers collection

Sammlung Philara
Birkenstraße 47a
40233 Düsseldorf
www.philara.de
info@philara.de
+49 (0) 211 24 86 27 21

Öffnungszeiten
Opening Hours
FR 16–20 Uhr 4–8 pm
SA 14–18 Uhr 2–6 pm
SO 14–18 Uhr 2–6 pm
Pay what you wish

Künstlerische Direktion
Artistic Director
Julika Bosch

Sammlungsbetreuung, Registrar
Collection Management, Registrar
Ruben Benjamin Smulczynski

Eventmanagement Event Managment
Benita von Puttkamer

Kuratorin Curator
Hannah Niemeier

Kuratorische Assistenz
Curatorial Assistance
Dana Magarete Adele Bulic

Praktikum Internship
Nika Fateh

Vermittlung Guided Tours
Banu Alpsü, Stefan Bauer,
Christina Brikmann, Simon Ertel,
René Gipperich, Mara Vieten

Empfang Front Desk
Stefan Bauer, René Gipperich,
Maxi Lorenz

Ausstellungstechnik Technical Team
Frederic Bahr, Nico Flies,
Sonja Heim, Min-Hae Sohn

Haustechnik Building Services
Kalle Lenders

Licht-, Ton- und Videotechnik
Lights, Sound and Video
Fred Flor

Gestaltung Design
Laura Catania, Thomas Spallek

Impressum Imprint

Dieser Katalog erscheint anlässlich der Ausstellung This catalogue is published on the occasion of the exhibition

See Yourself as Lovers See You
William N. Copley | Dorothy Iannone
13.8.2023–14.1.2024

Herausgeberinnen Editors
Julika Bosch, Hannah Niemeier
Sammlung Philara

Kuratorin Curator
Julika Bosch

Kuratorische Assistenz
Curatorial Assistance
Dana Magarete Adele Bulic

Wissenschaftliche Mitarbeit
Research Fellow
Hannah Niemeier

Autor*innen Authors
Anthony Atlas
Florence Bonnefous
Julika Bosch

Lektorat Editing
Katharina Freisinger
Anna Grant

Übersetzung (DE) Translation (GER)
Katharina Freisinger

Übersetzung (EN) Translation (ENG)
Anna Grant

Gestaltung Design
Laura Catania

Gesamtherstellung Production
Druckerei Kettler, Bönen

Erschienen im Published by
Verlag Kettler, Dortmund
www.verlag-kettler.de

ISBN: 978-3-98741-172-4

Abbildungsnachweis Photo Credits
© The Estate Of Dorothy Iannone
© The Estate of William N. Copley
VG Bild-Kunst, Bonn
Photo: Kai Werner Schmidt, Susanne Diesner, Sammlung Philara

Copyright
© 2024 Sammlung Philara Philara Collection und die Autor*innen and the authors

Dank Acknowledgements
Familie Bronner
Bronner Family
Stiftung Ahlers Pro Arte
Ahlers Pro Arte Foundation
Air de Paris, Paris
The Estate Of Dorothy Iannone, Florence Bonnefous
The Estate of William N. Copley, Anthony Atlas
Galerie Friese, Klaus Gerrit Friese
Linn Lühn, Düsseldorf
Peres Projects, Berlin
Privatsammlung Private collection
Privatsammlung Private collection NRW
Stiftung Foundation Der Bewohnte Garten, Christina Wimmer und Michael Zimmer
Barbara Wien